THE VICTORIOUS KINGDOM MARRIAGE MANUAL

A MANUAL FOR A VICTORIOUS KINGDOM MARRIAGE

"FOR THIS CAUSE SHALL A MAN LEAVE HIS FATHER AND MOTHER, AND SHALL BE JOINED UNTO HIS WIFE, AND THEY TWO SHALL BE ONE FLESH. THIS IS A GREAT MYSTERY: BUT I SPEAK CONCERNING CHRIST AND THE CHURCH" (EPHESIANS 31-32).

WRITTEN BY:

APOSTLE BARNABAS GBEINTOR AND PROPHETESS VICTORIOUS GBEINTOR

PUBLISHED BY:

Raymond Business Focus

COPYRIGHT

Copyright © 2024 Apostle Barnabas and Prophetess Victorious Gbeintor

All rights reserved. No part of this publication may be reproduced, distributed, or transmitted in any form or by any means, including photocopying, recording, or other electronic or mechanical methods, without the prior written permission of the publisher, except in the case of brief quotations embodied in critical reviews and certain other noncommercial uses permitted by copyright law.

For permission requests, write to the publisher at the address below: Apostle Barnabas Gbeintor
2402 7th Ave North Fargo ND 58102
Riveroflife2016@gmail.com

SCRIPTURE QUOTATIONS
Scripture quotations are taken from the Bible:

DISCLAIMER

The information presented in this book is intended for the purpose of kingdom education and spiritual growth of every kingdom citizen, child of the King Creator, Lord Jesus Christ. Readers are encouraged to seek the guidance of the Holy Spirit before applying any principles or making decisions based on the content of this book.

SPECIAL BOOKING INFORMATION

This publication is available in print and electronic formats.

First Edition: September 2024

For bulk orders or to book a special marriage event, seminar, or conference in your area, please contact.
Kingdomschoolnd@gmail.com or riveroflife2016@gmail.com

(602)483 9552

All rights reserved.

Dedication

We humbly dedicate this priceless book and ministry to everyone who has ever been told that they could not achieve their dreams. To all the married couples who have weathered the storms of life and continue to forge ahead, striving for even greater glory—we honor your resilience and unwavering faith.

This book is dedicated to the generation of married couples who will leave an indelible mark on their time, allowing the Kingdom of Heaven to be manifested through their marriages. Your commitment to live out God's divine purpose through your union is both inspiring and transformative.

We also dedicate this book to the fathers and mothers who will take a bold stand, allowing their families to be used by Heaven as a kingdom model in their churches, communities, and across the world. Your legacy of faith and leadership will shine as a beacon for others to follow.

To the newlyweds, we dedicate this book with the hope that you will make a deliberate effort to seek the knowledge of God, nurturing and preserving your marriage as you grow together in love and faith. Your intentional pursuit of God's wisdom will be the foundation upon which your marriage flourishes.

We dedicate this book to our publishing company, Raymond Business Focus, for their outstanding kingdom services, unwavering encouragement, and steadfast confidence in us. Your commitment to excellence has been instrumental in bringing this essential marriage tool to life in a timely and professional manner. We are deeply grateful for your partnership in this endeavor and for your role in helping us fulfill our mission.

Acknowledgement

We are deeply privileged and honored to express our heartfelt gratitude to the Highest God, King Jesus Christ, for instilling in us the passion and for counting us worthy to represent His holy institution of marriage in our generation. Thank you, Lord, for choosing and anointing us with the wisdom and patience to surrender our marriage as a model of Your Kingdom.

We extend our sincere thanks to our River of Life Church family, both in Fargo, ND, and in Nimba County, Liberia. Your unwavering support and prayers have been a cornerstone in our journey.

We also wish to express our deepest appreciation to all the wonderful couples—past, present, and future—whom the Lord has blessed us to join in their wedding celebrations and to walk alongside in their marriage journeys. Your stories of love and commitment inspire us daily.

Finally, we acknowledge and thank all our social media couples and supporters across every platform where the Victorious Kingdom Marriage Weekly Show is broadcast. Your encouragement and engagement empower us to continue this ministry with joy and purpose. Finally, we are honored to acknowledge the Lord's kingdom Ambassador, our beloved brother, and kingdom partner, Pastor Oliver N. Giddings and his wonderful Liberty kingdom Chapel family in Fargo ND.

Table of contents

Dedication 4

Acknowledgement 5

Table of contents 6

Preface 9

Introduction 10

How to use the manual 11

The foundation of the kingdom marriage 13

    Chapter one

    BIBLICAL FOUNDATIONS OF MARRIAGE 15

Understanding God's Design for Marriage 16

BIBLICAL FOUNDATIONS OF MARRIAGE 16

        Roles and Responsibilities in Marriage 20

        The Order of Marriage 22

        UNDERSTANDING HEADSHIP AND SUBMISSION 22

    Chapter Two 28

Building a Strong Spiritual Foundation 28

The Power of Prayer in Marriage 28

        Studying Scripture Together 30

        THE IMPORTANCE OF STUDYING THE HOLY SCRIPTURES TOGETHER. 30

The Essential of Faith on the Marriage Journey 33

        Worship and fellowship as a couple 34

        DEFINITION OF WORSHIP AND FELLOWSHIP 34

- Chapter Three 40
- Communication and Conflict Resolution 40
- Principles of Effective Communication in Marriage 40
  - Listening with Love and Understanding 42
  - DEFINITION OF ACTIVE LISTENING 42
  - Cultivating a Culture of Forgiveness in Marriage 44
  - DEFINITION OF FORGIVENESS 44
- Resolving Conflicts Biblically 47
- Qualities of a Godly Couple 49
  - QUALITIES OF A HUSBAND 49
  - QUALITIES OF GODLY A WIFE 51
- Chapter Four 54
- Love, Respect, and Intimacy 54
- Understanding the Biblical Concept of Love 54
  - The Role of Respect in a Healthy Marriage 55
  - DEFINITION OF RESPECT 55
  - CULTIVATING A CULTURE OF RESPECT IN MARRIAGE 57
  - God's Design for Marital Intimacy 58
  - DEFINITION AND IMPORTANCE OF MARITAL INTIMACY 58
  - The Battle of Rulership 60
  - YOU ASK WHAT IS THIS POSITION? 61
- Chapter Five 70
- Financial Stewardship in Marriage 70
- BIBLICAL PRINCIPLES OF MONEY MANAGEMENT 70
  - PRACTICAL STEPS FOR BIBLICAL MONEY MANAGEMENT 71
  - Creating a Budget Together 72
  - Generosity and Giving as a Couple 74
  - DEFINITION AND IMPORTANCE 74
  - TITHES AND OFFERINGS 75
  - THE FOUNDATION OF FINANCIAL STEWARDSHIP 75

- Chapter Six 80
- Parenting And Family Life 80
- Raising Children in a Godly Home 80
- PRACTICAL STRATEGIES FOR BALANCING MARRIAGE AND PARENTING 82
  - Uniformity in Parenting a Blended Family 84
  - HOW TO PARENT A BLENDED FAMILY IN MARRIAGE? 84
- BUILDING A LEGACY OF FAITH 86
  - Chapter Seven 90
- Facing Trials and Growing Together 90
- Trusting God in Difficult Times 90
  - Strengthening Your Marriage Through Adversity 91
  - THE INEVITABILITY OF ADVERSITY 91
  - Encouraging Each Other's Spiritual Gifts 93
  - UNDERSTANDING SPIRITUAL GIFTS 93
  - Chapter Eight 98
- Serving God and Renewing Commitment 98
- Finding Your Joint Ministry 98
  - Serving in the Church and Community 100
  - THE CALL TO SERVE 100
  - Renewing Your Vows and Commitment 103
  - THE IMPORTANCE OF RENEWAL 103
  - Conclusion 108
- Embracing the Journey 108
- Scriptural Prayers for Couples to Pray Together 111

Preface

Marriage is a sacred covenant, a divine institution established by God to reflect His love and glory on earth. In a world where the sanctity of marriage is often challenged, it is more important than ever for couples to anchor their relationships in biblical truth and godly principles. This book is written to guide couples on a journey of spiritual growth, emotional intimacy, and practical wisdom, rooted in the Word of God.

Every chapter is designed to address the various aspects of married life, from understanding the divine roles of husband and wife to managing finances, nurturing intimacy, and raising a godly family. The book also highlights the importance of prayer, humility, and mutual respect, providing scriptural prayers and insights that couples can use to strengthen their bond.

We live in a fast-paced, technology-driven world where the distractions are many and the pressures are great. It is easy for couples to drift apart, to lose sight of the sacredness of their union. This book serves as a reminder that marriage is not just a contract but a covenant—one that requires commitment, sacrifice, and a daily surrender to God's will.

Whether you are newlyweds or have been married for decades, this book is a resource to help you navigate the challenges of marriage with grace and faith. It is our prayer that as you read and apply the principles found in these pages, your marriage will not only survive but thrive, becoming a beacon of hope and a testimony to the power of God's love.

May the Lord bless your marriage, enrich your love, and guide you as you walk this journey together for His kingdom expression in the earth.

Introduction

The "Victorious Kingdom Marriage Manual" addresses a series of profound questions that resonate with people worldwide. It serves as a comprehensive solution to the pervasive issues surrounding marriage, which seem to be influenced by the adversarial forces that seek to undermine this sacred institution. The manual explores crucial questions such as: Why does the enemy harbor such animosity towards marriage? Why are marriages increasingly failing and becoming subjects of ridicule in contemporary society? Why is the definition of marriage being altered? Why are more individuals reluctant to consider the necessity of having a spouse? What causes newlyweds to head towards divorce within their first year of marriage?

The manual also delves into why marriages are struggling even within the church community. It questions why couples, who should ideally be content, find themselves repeatedly committing adultery. It seeks to understand why many married individuals lack the knowledge or understanding of how to sustain their marriage. Moreover, it contemplates the true essence of marriage itself.

In response to these pressing questions, the Creator and Designer of Marriage has provided this manual as a means to reclaim, restore, and empower His creation in our generation. Through this manual, readers will gain practical insights into how to function effectively within the holy institution of marriage and fulfill the divine will. It aims to equip individuals with the necessary tools to thrive in their marital relationships, ensuring that marriage is not only sustained but flourishes by its intended purpose.

How to use the manual

The "Victorious Kingdom Marriage Manual" is designed to be a comprehensive guide that provides practical insights and solutions for nurturing a successful and fulfilling marriage. Here's how you can effectively use this manual

Read Thoroughly: Begin by reading the manual from start to finish to understand its overall message and themes. This will give you a holistic view of the principles and strategies it advocates.

Reflect on Key Questions: Reflect on the key questions posed in the manual, such as why marriages are failing, why the enemy targets marriage, and why certain issues arise within marital relationships. Contemplate how these questions relate to your own experiences or observations.

Follow the Structure: The manual is likely organized into sections or chapters, each addressing different aspects of marriage. Follow this structure systematically, as each part builds upon the previous one, providing a comprehensive understanding of the subject.

Engage with Practical Advice: Pay close attention to the practical advice and strategies offered. These are designed to help you navigate common challenges and improve various aspects of your marriage. Take notes and highlight key points that resonate with you.

Apply the Principles: Actively apply the principles and strategies to your marriage. This may involve making changes to your behavior, communication style, or approach to conflict resolution. The manual is most effective when its teachings are put into practice. Knowledge is information, understanding is comprehension, and wisdom is when knowledge understood is applied.

Utilize Exercises and Activities: If the manual includes exercises, activities, or reflection questions, take the time to complete them. These are designed to deepen your understanding and help you internalize the lessons.

Discuss with Your Spouse: Share insights and discuss the manual's content with your spouse. Open communication about the manual's teachings can foster mutual understanding and cooperation in implementing the suggested practices.

Seek Guidance: If certain concepts or strategies are challenging to understand or apply, seek guidance from a trusted mentor, counselor, or spiritual advisor. They can provide additional perspective and support.

Review Regularly: Marriage is a dynamic relationship that evolves. Regularly review the manual to refresh your understanding and adjust your practices as needed.

Stay Committed: Commit to continuous improvement and growth in your marriage. The manual is a tool for long-term success, so staying dedicated to its principles will yield the best results.

By following these steps, you can effectively utilize the "Victorious Kingdom Marriage Manual" to build a strong, resilient, and fulfilling marriage that aligns with the divine purpose.

The foundation of the kingdom marriage

A Kingdom marriage is one that aligns with God's divine purpose and reflects His glory. The foundation of such a marriage is built upon understanding and adhering to biblical principles, recognizing marriage as a sacred covenant, and committing to nurturing a relationship that honors God in every aspect. When the Creator originally wanted to influence the earth, He started with the husband and his wife, His human family. If the church today is called out to be the light in the darkness, or the solution to the pollution, then the church must make every effort to restore, and strengthen our marriages with sound doctrine because our marriages consist of the same people who are the body of Christ. Every church is only as good as their marriages, and families. The Lord does not want to do anything new concerning His marriage product, He is only urging the body of Christ to focus more on restoring, and empowering His original vehicle called marriage to rise to the occasion in our generation to express His nature and character. The soundness of the human family is the key to showcasing the glory of the Lord in every generation until Jesus returns.

Prov 19:21 A man's heart may be full of designs, but the purpose of the Lord is unchanging.

Biblical Foundations of Marriage: At the core of a Victorious Kingdom marriage is the understanding that marriage was instituted by God and is designed to mirror the relationship between Christ and the Church. This sacred union is not just a social contract but a divine covenant meant to showcase God's love, unity, and purpose through the human family. By studying the holy Scriptures, couples can gain a deeper understanding of God's design for marriage and the roles He has established for husbands and wives.

The Covenant Relationship: Marriage, in the Kingdom context, is a covenant—a solemn agreement that goes beyond a legal contract. This covenant is a lifelong commitment that reflects God's unbreakable promise to His people. Understanding marriage as a covenant means recognizing the seriousness of the commitment and the need for unwavering faithfulness, love, and support for one another.

Roles and Responsibilities in Marriage: A strong Kingdom marriage requires a clear understanding of the distinct roles and responsibilities assigned to each partner. The Bible outlines specific duties for husbands and wives, emphasizing mutual submission, respect, and love. Husbands are called to love their wives as Christ loves the Church, providing spiritual leadership and sacrificial care. Wives are called to respect and support their husbands, working together as partners to fulfill God's purpose for their marriage.

Spiritual Unity: Spiritual unity is a vital component of a Victorious Kingdom marriage. This involves growing together in faith, encouraging each other's spiritual growth, and maintaining a Christ-centered relationship. Praying together, studying the word of God, and participating in worship and fellowship are essential practices that strengthen the spiritual bond between spouses.

Commitment to Growth and Renewal: Building a Kingdom marriage requires a commitment to continuous growth and renewal. This involves regularly assessing the health of the marriage, seeking God's guidance, and making necessary adjustments to align with His will. Couples should strive to deepen their relationship with God and each other, always aiming to reflect His love and grace in their marriage.

By laying this strong foundation, couples can build a marriage that does not only endure but thrives, fulfilling God's purpose and bringing glory to His name. A Victorious Kingdom marriage is marked by agape love which is based on authentic biblical knowledge. The word of God makes us understand that it is not the lack of love that causes people to perish, but a lack of authentic knowledge or information. Love alone cannot preserve the marriage product, it is the intentional acquisition of the knowledge of the love of God, and studying to understand it to apply it to your marriage that can preserve it victoriously.

Hos 4:6 My people are destroyed for lack of knowledge; because thou hast rejected knowledge, I will also reject thee, that thou shalt be no priest to me: seeing thou hast forgotten the law of thy God, I will also forget thy children.

Married couples who are faithful, and committed to growing in the knowledge of God concerning marriage after their wedding will set themselves up for a victorious outcome. This shared strategy implemented by couples, and especially newlyweds, is the only way in which the husband and wife will be able to live out God's plan together for His kingdom expression and expansion on earth before all.

CHAPTER 1

Understanding God's Design for Marriage

BIBLICAL FOUNDATIONS OF MARRIAGE

Chapter One
Understanding God's Design for Marriage
BIBLICAL FOUNDATIONS OF MARRIAGE

Marriage is an institution established by God with profound significance and purpose. The biblical foundation of marriage provides insight into its divine design and roles in reflecting God's image or character, and fulfilling His purpose. The following keys scriptures offer a comprehensive understanding of the biblical basis for marriage

CREATION OF MAN AND WOMAN:
The foundation of marriage begins with the creation of man and woman. According to *Genesis 1:26-27:* **"Then God said, 'Let Us make man in Our image, according to Our likeness; let them have dominion over the fish of the sea, over the birds of the air, and over the cattle, over all the earth and over every creeping thing that creeps on the earth."** Genesis 1:27: **"So God created man in His image; in the image of God, He created him; male and female He created them."** This passage highlights that man and woman were created in the image of God, establishing the inherent dignity and value of both genders. Marriage, therefore, reflects the divine relationship and partnership intended by God between a husband and his wife. When a man and a woman come together to become one in body, soul, and spirit, this union is called marriage.

MARRIAGE AS A COVENANT:
Marriage is more than a contract; it is a sacred covenant instituted by God. In Genesis 2:24 (NKJV), the covenant nature of marriage is affirmed. *Genesis 2:24:* **"Therefore a man shall leave his father and mother and be joined to his wife, and they shall become one flesh."** This verse emphasizes the commitment and unity involved in marriage. The concept of becoming **"one flesh"** signifies a deep, intimate bond that is both physical and spiritual. It reflects a covenantal relationship characterized by faithfulness and mutual support.

THE ROLE OF MARRIAGE IN GOD'S PLAN
Marriage is designed to fulfill God's purposes on earth. In Malachi 2:15 (NKJV), the role of marriage in God's plan for human relationships is underscored. *Malachi 2:15:* **"But did He not make them one, having a remnant of the Spirit? And why one? He seeks godly offspring."** This verse indicates that marriage serves the purpose of producing godly offspring and maintaining a legacy of faithfulness. It underscores that marriage is part of God's larger plan for ensuring His teachings and values are passed down through generations.

MUTUAL SUBMISSION AND LOVE

The New Testament provides further insight into the nature of marital relationships through the teachings of the Apostle Paul. Ephesians 5:21-33 (NKJV) outlines the principles of mutual submission and love. *Ephesians 5:21:* **"Submitting to one another in the fear of God."** Ephesians 5:25: **"Husbands, love your wives, just as Christ also loved the church and gave Himself for her."** *E***phesians 5:21 Submitting yourselves one to another in the fear of God.** This passage teaches that marriage involves mutual submission and sacrificial love. Husbands are called to love their wives selflessly, as Christ loves the Church, while wives are encouraged to respect and support their husbands. This mutual submission reflects the selfless nature of God's love and provides a model for how couples should interact. Through our many marriages counseling and coaching experience, we have discovered that mutual submission remains the most difficult stage for many married couples. In an attempt to make couples understand the importance of mutual submission, It has been customary for me to teach mutual submission to couples by comparing the submission process to a 3 legged potato sack race where two people must place a leg into a sack while standing upright to race against their opponent who are also placed into the same position. Just like a 3-legged potato potato sack race, married couples must agree mutually to work together in all things. Couples should never waste precious time and energy on competing against one another but instead competing for each other. When mutual submission is not established quickly in the marriage, this refusal to mutually submit to one another in the fear of the Lord will become the contributing element that the enemy will use to hinder, abuse, delay, and attack the marriage. In a 3-legged potato sack race, the two couples in it must first agree to work together to put forth the intentional efforts, and strength one hop at a time until they have crossed the finish line together. Just like marriage, you will fall, crawl, argue, fight at times, but because you have determined in your mind to stay close no matter the storm, you two will continue fighting together until you have crossed the finish line. Marriage couples must always understand that marriage is not an institution for couples to compete against each other, but for couples to compete for each other every day in expressing the Lord's glory as they journey through life. Strive to always become the best team in every scenario life has to dish out. **Josh 23:10 One man of you shall chase a thousand: for the Lord your God, he [it is] that fighteth for you, as he hath promised you.**

I propose this question to every married couple: If one person can chase a thousand, how many do you think a husband and his wife can chase once they have established mutual submission in their marriage?

THE MARRIAGE RELATIONSHIP AS A REFLECTION OF CHRIST AND THE CHURCH

The relationship between husband and wife is intended to mirror the relationship between Christ and the Church. *Ephesians 5:32:* **"This is a great mystery, but I speak concerning Christ and the church."** This verse highlights that marriage is a profound symbol of Christ's relationship with the Church, emphasizing the importance of love, respect, and devotion within the marital relationship. It signifies that the marriage

17

relationship is not only a personal bond but also a reflection of divine truth and relationship.

ENDURING COMMITMENT AND FAITHFULNESS

Marriage is intended to be a lifelong commitment. In Matthew 19:6 (NKJV), Jesus reaffirms the indissolubility of marriage. *Matthew 19:6:* **"So then, they are no longer two but one flesh. Therefore, what God has joined together, let not man separate."** This passage reinforces that marriage is a divine union that should not be easily dissolved. It underscores the importance of maintaining faithfulness and commitment within the marriage covenant.

In summary, the biblical foundations of marriage emphasize its divine origin, covenantal nature, and role in fulfilling God's purposes. By understanding and adhering to these principles, couples can build a marriage that reflects God's image and aligns with His will.

The Covenant Relationship

Marriage, as described in the Bible, is a profound covenant relationship that transcends mere legal or social agreements. This covenantal view of marriage highlights its sacred nature and the deep, enduring commitment it entails. Here's a detailed exploration of the covenant relationship in marriage, with references to relevant scriptures

DEFINITION OF A COVENANT

A covenant is a solemn, binding agreement that establishes a deep and lasting relationship. Unlike a contract, which may be transactional and temporary, a covenant involves a mutual commitment to uphold certain promises and responsibilities. In the context of marriage, this covenant is established by God and is characterized by unconditional love, faithfulness, and permanence.

MARRIAGE AS A DIVINE COVENANT

The concept of marriage as a covenant is rooted in Scripture. In Malachi 2:14 (NKJV), God speaks about the covenant aspect of marriage. Malachi 2:14: "Yet you say, 'For what reason?' Because the Lord has been witnessing between you and the wife of your youth, with whom you have dealt treacherously; yet she is your companion and your wife by covenant." This passage emphasizes that marriage is a covenant witnessed by God. It highlights the seriousness of this divine agreement and the expectation of faithfulness within it. The idea is that marriage is not merely a human contract but a sacred bond established by God.

COMMITMENT AND FAITHFULNESS

A key feature of the covenant relationship in marriage is the commitment and faithfulness required. Jesus reinforces this understanding in Matthew 19:4-6, Matthew 19:4-6: **"And He answered and said to them, 'Have you not read that He who made them at the beginning 'made them male and female,' and said, 'For this reason a man shall leave his father and mother and be joined to his wife, and the two shall**

become one flesh'? So then, they are no longer two but one flesh. Therefore, what God has joined together, let not man separate."** This passage reflects the permanence of the marital covenant. Jesus reaffirms that marriage is a divine union that should not be broken by human intervention. The "one flesh" concept signifies an inseparable bond, reinforcing the idea of lifelong commitment. The lack of this profound truth in the minds of couples entering the institution of marriage is the primary reason why the divorce rate continues to increase both in and outside the church. Getting a divorce has become as easy as changing
an outfit in our society. As "Dr. Myles Monroe stated" if you do not know the purpose of a thing, abuse is inevitable. "

MUTUAL PROMISES AND RESPONSIBILITIES

In a covenant relationship, both parties make mutual promises and assume responsibilities. Ephesians 5:25-28 (NKJV) outlines these promises and responsibilities within the marriage covenant. Ephesians 5:25: **"Husbands, love your wives, just as Christ also loved the church and gave Himself for her."** Ephesians 5:28: **"So husbands ought to love their own wives as their own bodies; he who loves his wife loves himself."** Husbands are called to love their wives selflessly and sacrificially, reflecting Christ's love for the Church. Wives are encouraged to respect and support their husbands, creating a harmonious and mutually supportive relationship. These responsibilities are integral to upholding the covenant relationship.

THE COVENANT AS A WITNESS TO GOD'S FAITHFULNESS

Marriage as a covenant relationship serves as a witness to God's faithfulness. Just as God remains faithful to His covenants with humanity, so should married couples uphold their commitments to each other. In 1 Corinthians 13:7 (NKJV), the nature of love, which is central to the covenant, is described. 1 Corinthians 13:7: **"Love bears all things, believes all things, hopes all things, endures all things."** This verse illustrates the enduring nature of love within the covenant. It underscores the idea that love in marriage involves bearing with each other, believing in one another, and enduring challenges together, reflecting God's unchanging love.

RESTORATION AND RENEWAL OF THE COVENANT

Even when challenges arise, the covenant relationship allows for restoration and renewal. In 2 Chronicles 7:14 (NKJV), God provides a promise for healing and restoration. 2 Chronicles 7:14: **"If My people who are called by My name will humble themselves, and pray and seek My face, and turn from their wicked ways, then I will hear from heaven, and will forgive their sin and heal their land."** This promise highlights that God is willing to restore relationships, including marriages, when repentance and humility are present. The covenant relationship in marriage can be renewed through commitment to prayer, seeking God's guidance, and working towards reconciliation.
In conclusion, the covenant relationship in marriage reflects a deep, divine commitment that mirrors God's own covenant with His people. Understanding and embracing this

covenantal nature helps couples build a strong, enduring marriage based on mutual promises, faithfulness, and a shared commitment to God's purposes.

Roles and Responsibilities in Marriage

In a kingdom marriage, roles and responsibilities are divinely appointed to foster harmony, love, and mutual support. Understanding and embracing these divine roles helps couples to stay in alignment with purpose to fulfill God's design for their union. Here's a detailed exploration of the roles and responsibilities within marriage, with references to relevant scriptures

1. HUSBAND'S ROLE AND RESPONSIBILITIES
   The Bible outlines specific responsibilities for husbands, emphasizing leadership, love, and provision.

- **Leadership and Headship:** Husbands are called to lead their families with integrity and wisdom, reflecting Christ's leadership over the Church. Ephesians 5:23 (NKJV): **"For the husband is head of the wife, as also Christ is head of the church; and He is the Savior of the body."** This passage underscores the husband's role as the head of the family, guiding and protecting his household in alignment with God's will.

- **Loving and Sacrificial Leadership:** Husbands are commanded to love their wives selflessly, as Christ loves the Church. Ephesians 5:25 (NKJV): **"Husbands, love your wives, just as Christ also loved the church and gave Himself for her."** This sacrificial love involves prioritizing the wife's well-being, nurturing her spiritually, emotionally, and physically.

- **Provision and Responsibility:** Husbands are responsible for providing for their families, ensuring their needs are met. 1 Timothy 5:8 (NKJV): **"But if anyone does not provide for his own, and especially for those of his household, he has denied the faith and is worse than an unbeliever."** This responsibility encompasses financial provision as well as creating a secure and stable environment for the family.

2. WIFE'S ROLE AND RESPONSIBILITIES
   The Bible highlights complementary responsibilities for wives, emphasizing support, respect, and nurturing.

- **Helper and Supporter:** Wives are called to be helpers and supporters to their husbands, working together to fulfill God's purpose for their marriage. Genesis 2:18 (NKJV): **"And the Lord God said, 'It is not good that man should be alone; I will make him a helper comparable to him."** This role involves assisting and encouraging the husband, contributing to the partnership's overall success.

- **Respect and Submission:** Wives are encouraged to respect and submit to their husbands, fostering a respectful and harmonious relationship. Ephesians 5:22-24 (NKJV): **"Wives, submit to your own husbands, as to the Lord. For the husband is head of the wife, as also Christ is head of the church; and He is the Savior of the body. Therefore, just as the church is subject to Christ, so let the wives be to their** own husbands in everything." Submission in this context is not about inferiority but about a willing, respectful partnership under the husband's loving leadership.

- **Nurturing and Managing the Home:** Wives often take on the role of nurturing and managing the household, ensuring a loving and supportive environment for the family. Proverbs 31:27-28 (NKJV): **"She watches over the ways of her household, and does not eat the bread of idleness. Her children rise up and call her blessed; her husband also, and he praises her."** This responsibility includes managing daily household tasks, nurturing children, and creating a home where love and faith can flourish. Though these are all duo responsibilities to be shared by both the husband and his wife, however wives are naturally anointed by the Lord from creation to help manage His purpose or divine assignment in the heart of their husbands.

3. MUTUAL RESPONSIBILITIES IN MARRIAGE

   Beyond individual roles, the Bible emphasizes mutual responsibilities that both husbands and wives should uphold.

- **Mutual Love and Respect:** Both spouses are called to love and respect each other, creating a foundation of mutual honor and care. Ephesians 5:33 (NKJV): **"Nevertheless let each one of you in particular so love his own wife as himself, and let the wife see that she respects her husband."** Mutual love and respect are crucial for maintaining a healthy, God-honoring marriage.

- **Partnership in Parenting:** Husbands and wives share the responsibility of raising their children in a godly manner, providing spiritual and moral guidance. Proverbs 22:6 (NKJV): **"Train up a child in the way he should go, and when he is old he will not depart from it."** This involves teaching children about God's ways, modeling Christian values, and nurturing their faith by living it out sincerely before them.

- **Spiritual Growth and Unity:** Both spouses should work together to grow spiritually, supporting each other in their faith journey. 1 Peter 3:7 (NKJV): **"Husbands, likewise, dwell with them with understanding, giving honor to the wife, as to the weaker vessel, and as being heirs together of the grace of life, that your prayers may not be hindered."** This mutual pursuit of spiritual growth fosters unity and strengthens the marriage bond.

4. BALANCING ROLES WITH FLEXIBILITY

   While the Bible provides clear roles and responsibilities, it also allows for flexibility and mutual support based on individual strengths and circumstances. Ecclesiastes 4:9-10 (NKJV): **"Two are better than one, because they have a good reward for their labor. For if they fall, one will lift up his companion."** Couples should communicate openly about their roles, supporting each other and adapting as needed to maintain a healthy, balanced partnership.

   In conclusion, understanding and embracing the biblical roles and responsibilities in marriage helps couples build a strong, harmonious relationship that reflects God's design. By committing to love, respect, support, and mutual growth, husbands and wives can fulfill their God-given purposes within their union.

The Order of Marriage
UNDERSTANDING HEADSHIP AND SUBMISSION

Marriage is a divine institution designed to reflect God's glory on earth through the human family. This chapter delves into the biblical principles of headship and submission, aiming to bring clarity and harmony to marriages. Understanding these principles helps couples navigate their roles and responsibilities, fostering a balanced and mutually respectful relationship.

THE CONCEPT OF HEADSHIP

The Bible outlines that the husband is the head of the wife, much like Christ is the head of the Church. Ephesians 5:23 states, **"For the husband is the head of the wife, as Christ also is the head of the church, He Himself being the Savior of the body."** This analogy highlights the husband's role as a leader who provides protection, guidance, and care for his family.

In our marriage, embracing the concept of headship has been crucial. As we united our families, I had to learn to lead with authority, tempered with love and compassion. My wife's trust and support in my leadership have been pivotal in maintaining our unity and strength as a family. Her encouragement and faith in me have empowered me to lead effectively and lovingly.

THE ROLE OF SUBMISSION

Submission, often misunderstood, is not about inferiority or losing one's identity. It is a voluntary act of respect and support for the husband's leadership. Ephesians 5:22 says, **"Wives, submit to your own husbands, as to the Lord."** This submission is a gesture of respect and trust, acknowledging the husband's role within the divine order of the family.

When we married, my wife brought four children into our union, and I brought four of my own. Her willingness to embrace her role with grace, strength, and humility, trusting in my leadership, has been fundamental in creating a harmonious and loving household. She has shown remarkable resilience and patience, fostering a nurturing environment for all our children.

MUTUAL LOVE AND RESPECT

The biblical model of marriage is a partnership built on mutual love and respect. While the husband is called to lead, he is also commanded to love his wife sacrificially as his leadership is authenticated by his expression of Christ's agape love shown for His church. I have personally learned from my journey to that every man must not enter their marriage attempting to find a shortcut

Ephesians 5:25 instructs, **"Husbands, love your wives, just as Christ loved the church and gave himself up for her."** This love is selfless, prioritizing the needs and well-being of the wife and family above his own.

Likewise, the wife's submission is not about blind obedience but about supporting her husband's role while maintaining her dignity and strength. Proverbs 31:10-12 describes a virtuous wife whose worth is far above rubies, whose husband safely trusts her, and who does him good and not evil all the days of her life.

ADDRESSING THE BATTLE OF POWER

One of the common challenges in many marriages is the struggle for power and control. Embracing the biblical order can help resolve these conflicts and establish a harmonious relationship. Here are some practical steps to apply these principles:

- **Open Communication:** Discuss your roles and expectations openly. Understand each other's perspectives and find common ground. Open dialogue fosters mutual understanding and respect.

- **Mutual Respect:** Respect each other's roles and contributions. Acknowledge and appreciate what each person brings to the marriage. Respect builds a strong foundation for a lasting relationship.

- **Shared Decision-Making:** While the husband may have the final say, it is important to make decisions together. Value each other's opinions and insights. Shared decision-making strengthens the partnership.

- **Love and Sacrifice:** Husbands should lead with love and selflessness, prioritizing the well-being of their wives and families. Wives should support their husbands with respect and trust. Love and sacrifice are the cornerstones of a thriving marriage.

- **Prayer and Spiritual Growth:** Pray together for wisdom and guidance. Seek to grow spiritually as a couple, allowing God to shape and strengthen your marriage. Spiritual growth fosters unity and resilience.

1 Peter 3:7 advises husbands to **"dwell with them with understanding, giving honor to the wife, as to the weaker vessel, and as being heirs together of the grace of life, that your prayers may not be hindered."** This scripture underscores the importance of making every effort to learn, understand, and honor each other, recognizing that both are equal heirs of God's grace.

The Bible provides numerous examples and teachings on the order of marriage. Colossians 3:18-19 instructs, **"Wives, submit to your own husbands, as is fitting in the Lord. Husbands, love your wives and do not be harsh with them."** These verses emphasize a balance of submission and love, ensuring that both partners fulfill their roles with respect and care.

Genesis 2:24 sets the foundation for marriage: **"Therefore a man shall leave his father and mother and be joined to his wife, and they shall become one flesh."** This unity is essential for the couple to function as a cohesive unit, reflecting God's design for marriage.

The biblical order of marriage, with the husband as the head and the wife in a supportive role, is designed to create harmony and balance within the family. When both spouses understand and embrace their roles with love and respect, they reflect the relationship between Christ and the Church, bringing glory to God through their union.

By focusing on mutual love, respect, and understanding, couples can overcome the battle of power and build a strong, unified marriage. Embracing these principles allows both partners to flourish, creating a loving and supportive environment for themselves and their children. The order of marriage, as intended by God, is not about dominance or submission but about partnership, love, and respect, fostering a harmonious and thriving relationship.

MARRIAGE AS A DIVINE INSTITUTION

Marriage, as conceived by God, is not merely a social contract or a convenient arrangement for companionship. It is a divine institution with a sacred purpose: to reflect God's glory on earth through the human family. This profound vision elevates the role of marriage far beyond human expectations, imbuing it with spiritual significance and eternal value.

THE DIVINE BLUEPRINT

The biblical account of creation provides the foundation for understanding marriage as a divine institution. In Genesis 1:27-28, God created mankind in His own image, male and female, and blessed them with the mandate to be fruitful and multiply, to fill the earth and subdue it. This creation narrative underscores that marriage is part of God's original design for humanity, meant to mirror His relational nature, creative, and influential power

Furthermore, Genesis 2:24 describes the union of husband and wife as becoming **"one flesh."** This union is a mystery that signifies a profound spiritual and physical bond, intended to reflect the unity and diversity within the Godhead. The intimate relationship between husband and wife is a living illustration of the relationship between Christ and His Church, as outlined in Ephesians 5:31-32.

HEADSHIP AND SUBMISSION: A BALANCED DESIGN

Understanding the principles of headship and submission is crucial for achieving clarity and harmony in marriage. These principles are not about hierarchy or dominance but about order and mutual respect, designed to foster a balanced and fulfilling relationship.

- **Headship**: Ephesians 5:23 states, **"For the husband is the head of the wife, as Christ is the head of the church, his body, of which he is the Savior."** This analogy emphasizes that the husband's role as the head is modeled after Christ's sacrificial leadership.

- **Leadership in Love**: The husband's headship involves leading with agape love, humility, and selflessness. It means providing spiritual guidance, protection, and provision for the family. This leadership is not about asserting authority but about serving and uplifting the wife and children, as Christ serves and uplifts the Church. Through my experience as a Shepherd at the River of life Church, I have encountered many husbands who entered their marriages driven to be recognized as the head or authority by their wives. One consistent quality in these husbands was that they were all failing to express the kind of character or behaviors to their wives which was worthy of receiving such a honor naturally from them. This on-going frustration built up in these husbands was real, but the sad reality was, they had no idea how to fix this stalemate in their marriages. I am also guilty of this error during my first 2 years of marriage until the Holy Spirit delivered me with this verse.

2Cor 10:18 For the Lord's approval of a man is not dependent on his opinion of himself, but on the Lord's opinion of him.

"The Lord spoke to my arrogant and hasty heart to not be so quick to assume a reward that I have not put forth the labor for."

The Lord made me understand that when I intentionally sow seeds of love and patience into my wife, He the (Lord) would touch her heart to respect or submit to me naturally without me forcing her to do so."

I remember saying the Lord after He spoke these thought-provoking words to me that "marriage was hard"

Then the Lord spoke softly into my spirit these precious words" Yes my son marriage is harder especially if you refuse to learn my love, and to love your wife like I so loved the world, and died for it."

Mt (BBE) 11:28 Come to me, all you who are troubled and weighed down with care, and I will give you rest.

Mt 11:29 Take my yoke on you and become like me, for I am gentle and without pride, and you will have rest for your souls;

- **Submission**: Ephesians 5:22 instructs, **"Wives, submit yourselves to your own husbands as you do to the Lord."** Submission is a voluntary act of respect and support, recognizing and honoring the husband's role.
- **Mutual Submission**: It is important to note that Ephesians 5:21 precedes this directive with a call to mutual submission: **"Submit to one another out of reverence for Christ."** This mutual submission establishes an environment of reciprocal love and respect, where both husband and wife seek each other's good.

NAVIGATING ROLES AND RESPONSIBILITIES
Embracing these principles helps couples navigate their roles and responsibilities with clarity and purpose. By understanding headship and submission within the context of love and mutual respect, couples can overcome common marital challenges and build a stronger, more unified relationship.

- **Shared Goals and Vision**: Couples should work together to establish shared goals and a unified vision for their marriage. This involves open communication, prayer, and seeking God's guidance in all aspects of their relationship. Shared goals and vision create a sense of purpose and direction, fostering unity and cooperation.

- **Complementary Roles**: Recognize and appreciate the unique strengths and contributions each partner brings to the marriage. The husband's leadership and the wife's supportive role are complementary, designed to work together in harmony. Embracing these roles allows each partner to thrive and contribute to the overall well-being of the family.

- **Conflict Resolution**: Understanding headship and submission can also provide a framework for resolving conflicts. When disagreements arise, couples can look to these principles for guidance, seeking to honor and respect each other while finding solutions that align with God's design for their marriage. Effective conflict resolution builds trust and strengthens the marital bond.

REFLECTING GOD'S GLORY

Ultimately, the purpose of marriage as a divine institution is to reflect God's glory on earth. This is achieved through the loving, respectful, and harmonious relationship between husband and wife, which serves as a testimony to the world of God's love and faithfulness.

In our journey, my wife and I have experienced the transformative power of embracing these biblical principles. By recognizing the divine purpose of our marriage and striving to reflect God's glory through our relationship, we have found deeper intimacy, greater unity, and a more profound sense of purpose. Our marriage has become a source of strength and inspiration, not only for us but also for our children, and community.

Understanding marriage as a divine institution designed to reflect God's glory provides a profound and inspiring perspective. By embracing the biblical principles of headship and submission, couples can navigate their roles and responsibilities with clarity, fostering a balanced and mutually respectful relationship. This divine blueprint for marriage not only strengthens the marital bond but also serves as a powerful testimony to God's love and faithfulness in the world.

CHAPTER 2

Building a Strong Spiritual Foundation

THE POWER OF PRAYER IN MARRIAGE

Chapter Two
Building a Strong Spiritual Foundation
The Power of Prayer in Marriage

A strong spiritual foundation is essential for a victorious kingdom marriage. At the heart of this foundation lies the power of prayer. Prayer is not just a ritual but a vital lifeline that connects couples to God and to each other, fostering unity, strength, and divine guidance in their relationship.

The Importance of Prayer in Marriage: Prayer is the cornerstone of a godly marriage. It invites God's presence and power into the relationship, enabling couples to navigate the challenges and joys of life together. When couples pray together, they align their hearts and minds with God's will, creating a spiritual bond that supernaturally strengthens their marriage. Matthew 18:19-20 (KJV) states: **Again, I say unto you, that if two of you shall agree on earth as touching anything that they shall ask, it shall be done for them of my Father which is in heaven. For where two or three are gathered together in my name, there am I in the midst of them.**

This passage underscores the power of unity in prayer. When husbands and wives come together in prayer, they invite the presence of God into their marriage, creating a strong spiritual connection that cannot easily be broken. No wonder the devil and his demons work so hard to keep the husbands and their wives divided on issues that could easily be resolved through a unified prayer time together.

Enhancing Communication Through Prayer: Effective communication is vital in marriage, and prayer enhances this communication by fostering a deeper connection. When couples pray together, they open their hearts, share their deepest concerns, and seek God's guidance. This practice builds humility, trust and transparency, helping to resolve conflicts and misunderstandings.

Praying together allows couples to express their fears, hopes, and dreams to one another in the presence of God. This level of openness and honesty is essential for building a strong emotional bond. It also helps couples to understand each other's perspectives and to support each other's spiritual growth.

Strengthening Emotional and Spiritual Intimacy: Prayer fosters emotional and spiritual intimacy between spouses. It allows them to support each other's spiritual growth, encourage one another in faith, and deepen their emotional connection. Praying together creates a safe space for sharing vulnerabilities and expressing gratitude, strengthening the marital bond by communicating and presenting every concern boldly before the Lord.

Heb 4:16 Let us therefore come boldly unto the throne of grace, that we may obtain mercy, and find grace to help in time of need.

1 Thessalonians 5:16-18 (KJV) states: **Rejoice evermore. Pray without ceasing. In everything give thanks: for this is the will of God in Christ Jesus concerning you.** Continuous prayer and thanksgiving create a positive atmosphere in the marriage, fostering a sense of peace and contentment. This spiritual practice helps couples to maintain a grateful attitude and to focus on the blessings in their lives, rather than dwelling on challenges.

Seeking God's Guidance and Wisdom: In marriage, couples face numerous decisions and challenges. Prayer is a powerful tool for seeking God's guidance and wisdom. By turning to God in prayer, couples acknowledge their dependence on Him and trust in His divine plan for their lives. This reliance on God brings clarity and direction, ensuring that decisions are made in alignment with His will. 1 John 5:14 And this is the confidence that we have in him, that, if we ask anything according to his will, he heareth us: James 1:5 (KJV) states: **If any of you lack wisdom, let him ask of God, that giveth to all men liberally, and upbraideth not; and it shall be given him.** Seeking God's wisdom through prayer helps couples to make decisions that honor Him and strengthen their marriage. It also provides a sense of peace and assurance, knowing that they are following God's plan for their lives.

Overcoming Challenges and Strengthening Resilience: Marriage is a journey filled with both blessings and trials. Prayer equips couples to face challenges with resilience and faith. By praying together, couples can find comfort, strength, and peace in God's promises, knowing that they are not alone in their struggles. Prayer also fosters forgiveness and grace, essential components in overcoming conflicts. Philippians 4:6-7 (KJV) states: **Be careful for nothing; but in everything by prayer and supplication with thanksgiving let your requests be made known unto God. And the peace of God, which passeth all understanding, shall keep your hearts and minds through Christ Jesus.**

In times of difficulty, prayer provides a source of comfort and strength. It helps couples to maintain their focus on God's promises and to trust in His plan, even when circumstances are challenging. James 5:16 **So then, make a statement of your sins to one another, and say prayers for one another so that you may be made well. The prayer of a good man is full of power in its working.**

Creating a Legacy of Faith: A marriage grounded in prayer sets a powerful example for future generations. By prioritizing prayer, couples model a life of faith and dependence on God, creating a legacy of spiritual devotion for their children and grandchildren. This legacy can inspire and guide future generations to build their own marriages on a strong spiritual foundation. It is absolutely breathtaking to experience our children come into our rooms during their bedtime offering to pray for us. There are no words to describe such a divine act, but this is the reality of mommy and daddy making prayer a culture within their marriage.

Deuteronomy 6:6-7 (KJV) states: **And these words, which I command thee this day, shall be in thine heart: And thou shalt teach them diligently unto thy children, and shalt talk of them when thou sittest in thine house, and when thou walkest by the way, and when thou liest down, and when thou risest up.**

By incorporating prayer into their daily lives, couples demonstrate the importance of a strong spiritual foundation to their children. This practice helps to instill a sense of faith and dependence on God in the next generation.

By embracing the power of prayer, couples can build a strong spiritual foundation for their marriage, drawing closer to each other and to God. Prayer is the lifeline that sustains, strengthens, and guides marriages, enabling them to reflect God's love and grace to the world.

Studying Scripture Together
THE IMPORTANCE OF STUDYING THE HOLY SCRIPTURES TOGETHER.

2Tim 3:16 **Every holy Writing which comes from God is of profit for teaching, for training, for guiding, for education in righteousness:**
2Tim 3:17 **So that the man of God may be complete, trained and made ready for every good work.**

Studying the word of God together is essential for couples who want to build a strong spiritual foundation in their marriage. It helps deepen their understanding of God's mind concerning His marriage product, and helps couples to align their lives according to His will. Through shared Bible studies, couples will grow spiritually and learn how to apply biblical principles to their daily lives. This shared spiritual journey not only strengthens their individual faith but also solidifies their bond as a married couple.

SOME IMPORTANCE WITH REFERENCE:

❖ STRENGTHENS SPIRITUAL BOND
Matthew 18:20: **For where two or three gather in my name, there am I with them.**
Ecclesiastes 4:12: **Though one may be overpowered, two can defend themselves. A cord of three strands is not quickly broken.**

❖ ENCOURAGES MUTUAL SUPPORT
Galatians 6:2: *Carry each other's burdens, and in this way, you will fulfill the law of Christ.*
James 5:16: **Therefore, confess your sins to each other and pray for each other so that you may be healed. The prayer of a righteous person is powerful and effective.**

❖ ENHANCES COMMUNICATION
Philippians 4:6-7: **Do not be anxious about anything, but in every situation, by prayer and petition, with thanksgiving, present your requests to God. And the peace of God, which transcends all understanding, will guard your hearts and your minds in Christ Jesus.**
Colossians 4:2: **Devote yourselves to prayer, being watchful and thankful.**

❖ INVITES GOD'S PRESENCE
Psalm 145:18: *The Lord is near to all who call on him, to all who call on him in truth.*
1 John 5:14: **This is the confidence we have in approaching God: that if we ask anything according to his will, he hears us.**

Lk 18:7 **And will not God do right in the cause of his saints, whose cries come day and night to his ears, though he is long in doing it?**

Psalm 119:105 (KJV) states: *Thy word is a lamp unto my feet, and a light unto my path.* This verse highlights the guiding power of God's Word. When couples study God's word together, they gain divine guidance that illuminates their path, ensuring that their decisions and actions are in line with God's purpose for their marriage.

DEVELOPING SPIRITUAL INTIMACY

Spiritual intimacy is a crucial aspect of a Victorious Kingdom marriage, and studying Scriptures together fosters this deep connection. By sharing their insights, reflections, and personal experiences with God's Word, couples create a deeper emotional and spiritual bond. This practice encourages open communication, vulnerability, and mutual growth in faith, making their relationship stronger and more resilient.

Hebrews 4:12 (KJV) states: For the word of God is quick, and powerful, and sharper than any two-edged sword, piercing even to the dividing asunder of soul and spirit, and of the joints and marrow, and is a discerner of the thoughts and intents of the heart." The transformative power of the word of God can bring couples in intimate fellowship with the Lord as they explore His profound truths together. This shared journey strengthens their bond and helps them to support each other's spiritual development from the spiritual empowerment acquired from God's word.

Jn 14:23 Jesus said to him in answer, if anyone has love for me, he will keep my words: and he will be dear to my Father; and we will come to him and make our living-place with him.

BUILDING A SHARED FOUNDATION OF BELIEFS AND VALUES

Studying the word of God together helps couples build a shared foundation of beliefs and values. This foundation is crucial for making decisions, resolving conflicts, and raising a family according to God's principles. A shared understanding of biblical truths ensures that couples are aligned in their faith and values, promoting unity and harmony in their marriage.

Amos 3:3 (KJV) states: **Can two walks together, except they be agreed?**
A shared understanding of Scripture ensures that couples are aligned in their faith and values, enabling them to walk together in unity. This alignment fosters a cohesive and harmonious marriage, grounded in God's truth.

John 8:31-32 **Then said Jesus to those Jews which believed in him, If ye continue in my word, [then] are ye my disciples indeed; And ye shall know the truth, and the truth shall make you free.**

ENCOURAGING ACCOUNTABILITY AND GROWTH

Psalms 119:11 Thy word have I hid in my heart, that I might not sin against thee.
When couples study God's word together, they hold each other accountable in their spiritual growth. This mutual accountability encourages consistency in Bible study, prayer, and the application of biblical principles. It also provides an opportunity for couples to challenge and inspire each other to live out their faith more fully in their marriages.

Proverbs 27:17 (KJV) states:**Iron sharpeneth iron; so a man sharpeneth the countenance of his friend.**

By reading and studying scriptures together, couples can sharpen each other's understanding and application of God's Word, promoting continuous spiritual growth and maturity.

APPLYING BIBLICAL PRINCIPLES TO DAILY LIFE

Studying, and reading Scriptures together equips couples with practical wisdom for daily life. It provides guidance on how to handle various aspects of marriage, including communication, conflict resolution, parenting, and financial stewardship. By applying biblical principles, couples can navigate life's challenges with grace and wisdom.

Prov 24:3 (KJV)Through wisdom is a house builded; and by understanding it is established:

Prov 24:4 And by knowledge shall the chambers be filled with all precious and pleasant riches.

Psalms 119:165 (KJV) **Great peace have they which love thy law: and nothing shall offend them.**

Isa 55:11 (BBE) So will my word be which goes out of my mouth: it will not come back to me with nothing done, but it will give effect to my purpose, and do that for which I have sent it.

The application of Scriptures is key to experiencing its transformative power. Couples who study and apply God's Word together can build a strong, victorious kingdom marriage that reflects God's dominance in their lives and community.

CREATING A LEGACY OF FAITH FOR FUTURE GENERATIONS

Couples who prioritize studying the word of God together set a powerful example for their children and future generations. This practice instills a love for God's Word and a commitment to living out biblical principles. It creates a legacy of faith that can inspire and guide future generations to build their own marriages on a strong spiritual foundation.

Deuteronomy 6:6-7 (KJV) states: **And these words, which I command thee this day, shall be in thine heart: And thou shalt teach them diligently unto thy children, and shalt talk of them when thou sittest in thine house, and when thou walkest by the way, and when thou liest down, and when thou risest up.**

Practical Steps for Studying Scripture Together

- **Schedule Regular Study Time**: Set aside a specific time each day or week for Bible study. Consistency is key to developing a strong spiritual foundation.

- **Choose a Bible Study Plan**: Select a Bible study plan or devotional that interests both partners. This could be a book of the Bible, a topical study, or a devotional guide which entails specific areas of concerns that are arising from within the marriage.

- **Discuss and Reflect**: After reading, discuss what you've learned. Share insights, ask questions, and reflect on how the Scripture applies to your lives.

- **Pray Together**: Begin and end your study time with prayer. Ask God for wisdom, understanding, and guidance as you delve into His Word.

- **Apply What You Learn**: Identify specific ways to apply the biblical principles you've studied to your marriage and daily life.

- **Journal Your Journey:** Keep a journal of your Bible study sessions. Record insights, answered prayers, and personal reflections to track your spiritual growth as a couple.

By committing to study Scriptures together, couples can build a strong spiritual foundation, fostering unity, spiritual growth, and a shared commitment to living out God's will in their marriage.Psalms 119:97 **O how love I thy law! it [is] my meditation all the day.**

The Essential of Faith on the Marriage Journey

Marriage is a sacred journey that requires unwavering faith—a faith that is nurtured and strengthened by a deep commitment to God's Word. Just as a garden requires care and attention, so too does a marriage require faith to flourish. Faith in marriage is not merely a hopeful sentiment; it is the cornerstone upon which the relationship is built and sustained.

Hebrews 11:1 tells us, "Now faith is the substance of things hoped for, the evidence of things not seen." In the context of marriage, faith serves as the unseen foundation that supports love, trust, and unity. It is not influenced by human opinions or circumstances; rather, it is a divine gift operated by God Himself.

FAITH IN MARRIAGE IS ESSENTIAL FOR SEVERAL REASONS:

- **Faith to Love:** Love in marriage is not always easy. There will be times when emotions waver, but it is faith that empowers us to love unconditionally. Just as David had already defeated Goliath in his heart before the stone ever left his sling, faith allows us to see victories in our marriage even before they manifest.

- **Faith to Trust:** Trust is the bedrock of any marriage, and it takes faith to trust one another fully. This faith is what moves mountains, as Jesus said in **Matthew 17:20, "If ye have faith as a grain of mustard seed... nothing shall be impossible unto you."** Trust built on faith enables couples to overcome doubts and insecurities, allowing them to move forward together with confidence.

- **Faith in Action:** Faith without works is dead (James 2:26). In marriage, this means actively living out the principles of faith by showing love, patience, and kindness even when it's difficult. Your actions, guided by faith, will speak volumes and contribute to the growth and strength of your relationship.

- **Faith in God's Process:** Often, we pray for immediate changes in our spouses, but true faith understands that God's transformation is a process. **Hebrews 6:19 describes this** hope as "an anchor of the soul, both sure and steadfast." Even when change is not immediately visible, faith assures us that God is at work in our marriage.

- **Faith in God's Order:** Even when a spouse falls short, faith reminds us of the divine order established by God. Ephesians 5:23 reinforces the headship of the husband under Christ. Faith helps us honor and respect this order, trusting that God is working in each of us through prayer and obedience.

- **Faith in Words:** The words we speak into our marriage have the power to shape our reality. **Proverbs 18:20 states, "A man's belly shall be satisfied with the fruit of his mouth; and with the increase of his lips shall he be filled."** In times of disagreement, the tongue can become a weapon, but faith-filled speech can bring healing and unity. James 3:8-12 reminds us of the power of the tongue, urging us to use it to bless and build up our spouse, rather than to curse and to tear down.

Marriage is indeed God's Garden, and just as a gardener plant seeds with faith in the harvest to come, so too must couples plant words of faith, love, and encouragement. The words you sow into each other will determine the fruit your marriage bears.

In conclusion, faith is not just a component of marriage—it is essential. It is the faith that transforms challenges into triumphs, disappointments into divine appointments, and trials into testimonies. As you journey together in faith, let your words, actions, and hearts be firmly rooted in the Word of God, trusting Him to bring forth a marriage that reflects His kingdom glory **Rom 10.17 So then faith [cometh] by hearing, and hearing by the word of God.**

Worship and fellowship as a couple
DEFINITION OF WORSHIP AND FELLOWSHIP

Worship is the act of showing reverence and adoration for God. The marriage institution itself was manufactured to worship King Jesus Christ by allowing His expression to flow through it. Such worship involves praising, thanking, and honoring God for who He is and what He has done. Worship can be expressed through various forms such as singing, prayer, reading Scriptures, and living a life that glorifies God.

Fellowship refers to the communal aspect of the faith where believers come together to support, encourage, and build each other up in kingdom knowledge and encouragements. It involves sharing life experiences, praying together, studying the Bible, and serving one another in love. Fellowship is essential for spiritual growth and maintaining a sense of community within the body of Christ.

ENGAGING IN WORSHIP AND FELLOWSHIP AS A COUPLE

Engaging in worship and fellowship as a couple is a vital component of building a strong spiritual foundation in marriage. This practice nurtures the spiritual connection between partners and aligns their hearts with God's will.

Here are the detailed aspects and benefits of worship and fellowship as a couple:

1. **CORPORATE WORSHIP**

   Hebrews 10:24-25: **"And let us consider how we may spur one another on toward love and good deeds, not giving up meeting together, as some are in the habit of doing, but encouraging one another—and all the more as you see the Day approaching."**
   Psalm 122:1: **"I rejoiced with those who said to me, 'Let us go to the house of the Lord."**

   Corporate worship involves attending church services together. It is an opportunity for couples to experience communal worship, listen to sermons, and participate in holy sacraments. Regular attendance in church services strengthens the couple's faith and provides a sense of belonging to a larger faith community.

   Acts 2:41 Then they that gladly received his word were baptized: and the same day there were added [unto them] about three thousand souls.

   Acts 2:42 And they continued steadfastly in the apostles' doctrine and fellowship, and in breaking of bread, and in prayers.

   The above verses shine light on the supernatural impact of corporate worship in the lives of believers in the early church. Believers experienced tremendous spiritual growth due to their commitment to the fellowship and the biblical teachings being effort by their spiritual leaders and faith community.

   BENEFITS

   - **Shared Spiritual Growth:** Experiencing worship together helps couples grow spiritually in unison, creating a shared spiritual journey.

   - **Encouragement and Accountability:** Being part of a faith community provides encouragement and accountability, helping couples stay committed to their spiritual practices.

   - **Exposure to Teaching and sound Doctrine:** Regular attendance allows couples to learn biblical teachings and understanding that can be discussed and applied in their daily lives.
     Luke 10:39 And she had a sister called Mary, which also sat at Jesus' feet, and heard his word.

     Luke 10:42 But one thing is needful: and Mary hath chosen that good part, which shall not be taken away from her.

2. **PRIVATE WORSHIP**

   Psalm 34:3: **"Glorify the Lord with me; let us exalt his name together."**
   Ephesians 5:19: **"Speaking to one another with psalms, hymns, and songs from the Spirit. Sing and make music from your heart to the Lord."**

Private worship involves setting aside time to worship God together in the privacy of their home. This can include singing hymns, praying, reading Psalms, and reflecting on God's goodness in a private area of your home to worship together as a married couple. Private worship fosters a deep sense of spiritual intimacy and cultivation.

BENEFITS:

- **Spiritual Intimacy:** Engaging in private worship strengthens the spiritual bond between partners, fostering a deeper connection with God and each other.

- **Peace and Presence:** Regular private worship invites the peace and presence of God into the home, creating an atmosphere of spiritual tranquility.

- **Expression of Devotion:** It provides a space for couples to express their devotion to God together, reinforcing their faith and commitment.

3. SERVING TOGETHER

Galatians 5:13: **"You, my brothers and sisters, were called to be free. But do not use your freedom to indulge the flesh; rather, serve one another humbly in love."**

1 Peter 4:10: *"Each of you should use whatever gift you have received to serve others, as faithful stewards of God's grace in its various forms."*

Serving together in church or the community allows couples to live out their faith in practical ways. Whether it's volunteering, participating in outreach programs, or helping with church activities, serving together fosters a sense of purpose and unity.

BENEFITS:

- **Teamwork and Unity:** Serving together enhances teamwork and strengthens the unity of the marriage. It requires communication, collaboration, and mutual support.

- **Fulfillment of God's Command:** It fulfills God's command to serve others and demonstrate His love through actions.

- **Modeling Christ's Love:** Serving together models Christ's love and compassion, providing a powerful witness to others.

4. Fellowship with Other Believers

Acts 2:42: **"They devoted themselves to the apostles' teaching and to fellowship, to the breaking of bread and to prayer."**

Proverbs 27:17: **"As iron sharpens iron, so one person sharpens another."**

Fellowship with other believers involves building relationships with other Christian couples. This can include participating in small groups, attending Bible studies, or simply spending time with other couples who share similar faith values.

BENEFITS:

- **Mutual Encouragement:** Fellowship with other believers provides mutual encouragement and support, helping couples stay strong in their faith.

- **Accountability:** Being part of a faith community offers accountability, helping couples stay true to their commitments and spiritual goals.

- **Shared Wisdom and Experience:** Engaging with other couples who are of the household of God allows for the sharing of wisdom, experiences, and practical advice on maintaining a godly marriage.

PRACTICAL STEPS FOR WORSHIP AND FELLOWSHIP As A COUPLE

- *Schedule Regular Church Attendance:* Make attending church services together a priority. Choose a church where both partners feel spiritually fed and connected.

- *Create a Private Worship Routine:* set aside a specific time each week for private worship. This could be a designated evening or morning where you sing hymns, pray, and read the Bible together.

- *Find Service Opportunities:* Look for opportunities to serve together in your church or community. This could be volunteering at a local charity, helping with church events, or participating in mission trips.

- *Join a Small Group or Bible Study:* Join a small group or Bible study that is led by the Holy Spirit that includes other couples. This provides a platform for deeper fellowship, discussion, and mutual support.

- *Host or Attend Fellowship Gatherings*: Host or attend gatherings with other kingdom minded couples. This can be as simple as a dinner, a game night, or a prayer meeting.

By incorporating these practices into their marriage, couples can build a robust spiritual foundation that strengthens their relationship with each other and with God. Worship and fellowship as a couple not only enriches their spiritual lives but also provides a strong support system and community, enhancing their overall marital satisfaction and growth which is graciously beneficial to the Lord's purpose for it.

CHAPTER 3

Communication and Conflict Resolution

Principles of Effective Communication in Marriage

Chapter Three
Communication and Conflict Resolution
Principles of Effective Communication in Marriage

DEFINITION OF COMMUNICATION

Communication is the process of exchanging information, ideas, thoughts, and feelings between individuals through verbal or non-verbal methods. Effective communication involves active listening, empathy, and clarity to ensure that the message is understood as intended. In marriage, communication is the cornerstone of a healthy and thriving relationship. It allows couples to connect on a deeper level, resolve conflicts, and build mutual trust and understanding.

IMPORTANCE OF COMMUNICATION IN MARRIAGE

- **Building Trust and Intimacy**: Open and honest communication fosters trust between spouses. When couples share their thoughts, fears, and dreams, they build a deeper emotional connection leading to greater intimacy. **"Therefore, each of you must put off falsehood and speak truthfully to your neighbor, for we are all members of one body." - Ephesians 4:25.** In marriage, this means being honest with one another, which builds trust and unity.

- **Resolving Conflicts**: Effective communication helps in addressing misunderstandings and conflicts constructively. By expressing feelings and listening to each other, couples can find common ground and resolve issues amicably. **"A gentle answer turns away wrath, but a harsh word stirs up anger." - Proverbs 15:1.** Gentle communication can de-escalate conflicts and promote peace in marriage.

- **Enhancing Mutual Support**: Through communication, spouses can offer support and encouragement to one another. Sharing daily experiences, concerns, and joys helps in understanding each other's needs and providing the necessary support. **"Therefore encourage one another and build each other up, just as in fact you are doing." - 1 Thessalonians 5:11.** Mutual encouragement strengthens the marital bond.

- **Strengthening Unity and Partnership**: Communication ensures that both partners are on the same page regarding their goals, values, and plans. It helps in making joint decisions and working together towards common objectives. **"Two are better than one, because they have a good return for their labor: If either of them falls down, one can help the other up." - Ecclesiastes 4:9-10.** Working together in unity amplifies the strength of the marriage.

COMPONENTS OF EFFECTIVE COMMUNICATION

- **Active Listening**: This involves fully concentrating, understanding, responding, and remembering what the other person is saying. It requires putting aside distractions and focusing entirely on the speaker. **"My dear brothers and sisters, take note of this:**

Everyone should be quick to listen, slow to speak and slow to become angry." - James 1:19. Being quick to listen and slow to speak fosters better understanding.

- **Empathy**: Empathy is the ability to understand and share the feelings of another. In marriage, empathizing with your spouse's emotions and perspectives shows compassion and care. **Rejoice with those who rejoice; mourn with those who mourn." - Romans 12:15.** Sharing in your spouse's joys and sorrows strengthens emotional bonds.

- **Clarity and Honesty**: Clear and honest communication avoids misunderstandings. It involves expressing thoughts and feelings in a straightforward manner while being respectful and considerate. **"Let your conversation be always full of grace, seasoned with salt, so that you may know how to answer everyone." - Colossians 4:6.** Speaking with grace and clarity promotes positive interactions.

- **Non-Verbal Communication**: Body language, facial expressions, and tone of voice also play a crucial role in communication. Non-verbal cues can reinforce or contradict what is being said, so it is important to be aware of them. **"The heart of the wise makes his speech judicious and adds persuasiveness to his lips." - Proverbs 16:23.** Wise and thoughtful non-verbal communication enhances the message being conveyed.

COMMUNICATION CHALLENGES AND SOLUTIONS IN MARRIAGE

- **Misunderstandings and Assumptions**: Misunderstandings can arise when messages are not clearly conveyed or received. Avoid making assumptions about your spouse's thoughts or intentions.

- **Solution**: Seek clarification by asking questions and restating what you heard to ensure accuracy. This helps in clearing up any confusion.

- **Emotional Barriers**: Negative emotions like anger, resentment, or fear can hinder effective communication. These emotions can lead to defensive or aggressive behavior.

- **Solution**: Practice emotional regulation and approach conversations with a calm and open mind. Use "I" statements to express feelings without blaming the other person (e.g., "I feel hurt when...").

- **Lack of Time and Attention**: Busy schedules and distractions can prevent meaningful communication.

- **Solution**: Set aside dedicated time for uninterrupted conversations. Prioritize regular check-ins to stay connected and address any issues promptly.

- **Differences in Communication Styles**: Individuals may have different ways of expressing themselves, which can lead to misunderstandings.

- **Solution**: Recognize and respect each other's communication styles. Adapt your approach to meet your spouse's needs, and work towards finding a common ground.

PRACTICAL STEPS FOR IMPROVING COMMUNICATION

- **Daily Check-Ins**: Spend a few minutes each day discussing your day, sharing thoughts, and expressing gratitude. This keeps the lines of communication open and builds a habit of connecting regularly.

- **Conflict Resolution Strategies**: Develop strategies for handling conflicts, such as taking breaks when emotions run high, and revisiting the issue with a calm and clear mind.

- **Marriage Counseling**: Seek professional help if communication issues persist. A kingdom minded marriage counselor can provide unbiased tools and techniques to improve communication and resolve conflicts in the manner that is pleasing unto the Lord.

- **Prayer and Scripture Study**: Incorporate prayer and scripture study into your daily routine. Praying together and studying the Bible can provide divine guidance and strengthen your spiritual connection.

"Call me and I will answer you and tell you great and unsearchable things you do not know." - Jeremiah 33:3. Seeking God's wisdom through prayer can enhance understanding and communication in marriage.

Effective communication is the lifeblood of a strong and healthy marriage. By investing in good communication practices, couples can navigate challenges, deepen their connection, and build a relationship that glorifies the Lord wholeheartedly.

Listening with Love and Understanding
DEFINITION OF ACTIVE LISTENING

Active listening is the intentional effort to understand your spouse's message by fully concentrating, understanding, responding, and remembering what is being said. This form of listening goes beyond merely hearing words; it involves engaging with the speaker to grasp the underlying emotions and intentions. Active listening requires empathy, patience, and the ability to put aside personal biases and distractions to truly understand the other person.

IMPORTANCE OF ACTIVE LISTENING IN MARRIAGE

- **Fosters Intimacy:** When you listen attentively, you show your spouse that you value their thoughts and feelings. This respect and validation deepen emotional intimacy and trust within the relationship.

"My dear brothers and sisters, take note of this: Everyone should be quick to listen, slow to speak and slow to become angry." - James 1:19. Quick listening and slow speaking foster intimacy, as they prevent hasty judgments and promote understanding.

- **Reduces Conflicts:** By understanding your spouse's perspective, you can prevent misunderstandings and resolve conflicts more effectively. This understanding helps in addressing the root cause of disagreements rather than just the symptoms.
  "A gentle answer turns away wrath, but a harsh word stirs up anger." - Proverbs 15:1. Gentle responses, facilitated by active listening, reduce conflicts and promote harmony.

- **Builds Trust**: Being a good listener builds trust and shows that you value your spouse's thoughts and feelings. Trust is the foundation of a strong and healthy marriage.
  "The heart of the discerning acquires knowledge, for the ears of the wise seek it out." - Proverbs 18:15. Wise listening builds trust and understanding, which are essential for a strong relationship.

- **Enhances Problem-Solving**: Understanding each other's viewpoints enables effective problem-solving and decision-making. When both partners feel heard and understood, they are more likely to work together towards common solutions.
  Plans fail for lack of counsel, but with many advisers they succeed." - Proverbs 15:22. Effective problem-solving requires understanding and counsel, which are facilitated by active listening.

PRACTICAL STEPS FOR ACTIVE LISTENING

- **Show Empathy**: Try to understand your spouse's feelings and perspective. Empathy involves putting yourself in their shoes and responding with compassion.

- **Avoid Interrupting**: Let your spouse finish speaking before responding. Interrupting can make them feel unheard and disrespected.

- **Summarize and Reflect**: Repeat back what you've heard to ensure understanding. This technique, known as reflective listening, shows that you are actively engaged in the conversation.

- **Ask Open-Ended Questions**: Encourage your spouse to share more about their thoughts and feelings. Open-ended questions cannot be answered with a simple "yes" or "no," prompting more detailed responses.

- **Be Patient**: Give your spouse your full attention and be patient, allowing them to express themselves fully without feeling rushed or misunderstood.

- **Validate Feelings**: Take the time to acknowledge your spouse's emotions and validate their feelings. This does not mean you have to agree with everything they say, but it shows that you recognize their emotional experience.

CHALLENGES AND OVERCOMING THEM

- **Personal Biases**

  Challenge: Personal biases and preconceived notions can hinder active listening.

  Solution: Approach conversations with an open mind, setting aside judgments and focusing on understanding your spouse's perspective.

  "Do not judge, or you too will be judged." - Matthew 7:1. Avoiding judgment helps in listening with an open heart.

- **Distractions**
  Challenge: External distractions can disrupt active listening.

  Solution: Create a conducive environment for conversations by eliminating distractions and focusing solely on your spouse.

  "Be still, and know that I am God." - Psalm 46:10. Stillness and focus are important for deep listening.

- **Emotional Reactions**
  Challenge: Strong emotional reactions can impede listening.

  Solution: Practice emotional regulation and respond calmly. Take a moment to breathe and collect your thoughts before responding.

  "The one who has knowledge uses words with restraint, and whoever has understanding is even-tempered." - Proverbs 17:27. Being even-tempered aids in effective communication.

- **Preoccupation with Response**
  Challenge: Focusing on what you will say next rather than listening to your spouse.

  Solution: Concentrate on your spouse's words and wait until they have finished speaking before formulating your response.

  Prov 18:13 (BBE) To give an answer before hearing is a foolish thing and a cause of shame.

  "Let your conversation be always full of grace, seasoned with salt, so that you may know how to answer everyone." - Colossians 4:6. Graceful conversation involves active listening.

Listening with love and understanding is crucial for building a strong, healthy marriage. The flesh will always suggest to our minds the need to defend ourselves when our spouses are addressing their concerns. The tendency to interrupt our spouse when he or she is expressing themselves is a reality. The need to present our own version of what we are being accused of exists, but this tactic has proven to not be a winning formula in marriage, as it only makes things worse. By practicing active listening through the enabling of the Holy Spirit, you show respect, empathy, and commitment to your spouse's thoughts. This fosters emotional intimacy, reduces conflicts, builds trust, and enhances problem-solving. Embrace the principles of active listening, overcome the challenges, and watch your marriage relationship grow stronger and more fulfilling.

Cultivating a Culture of Forgiveness in Marriage
DEFINITION OF FORGIVENESS

Forgiveness is the deliberate decision to release feelings of resentment or vengeance towards a person who has harmed you, regardless of whether they deserve it. It involves letting go of grudges and moving towards reconciliation and peace. In marriage, forgiveness is crucial for maintaining a healthy relationship. It allows couples to overcome conflicts, heal emotional wounds, and grow stronger together. **Rom 12:21 Be not overcome of evil, but overcome evil with good.**

IMPORTANCE OF FORGIVENESS IN MARRIAGE

- **Promotes Healing and Reconciliation**: Forgiveness helps in healing emotional wounds caused by misunderstandings or conflicts. It paves the way for reconciliation and rebuilding trust. **"Bear with each other and forgive one another if any of you has a grievance against someone. Forgive as the Lord forgave you."** - Colossians 3:13. Just as God forgives us, we are called to forgive our spouses, fostering healing and unity.

- **Breaks the Cycle of Resentment**: Holding onto grudges creates a cycle of resentment and bitterness, which can poison the relationship. Forgiveness breaks this cycle and restores peace. **"Get rid of all bitterness, rage and anger, brawling and slander, along with every form of malice. Be kind and compassionate to one another, forgiving each other, just as in Christ God forgave you."** - Ephesians 4:31-32. Letting goes of bitterness and embracing forgiveness leads to a healthier marriage.

- **Enhances Emotional Intimacy**: Forgiveness opens the door to deeper emotional intimacy. It allows couples to be vulnerable and honest with each other, strengthening their bond. **"Above all, love each other deeply, because love covers over a multitude of sins." - 1 Peter 4:8.** Deep love, characterized by forgiveness, fosters a strong emotional connection.

- **Reflects God's Love and Grace**: Forgiving your spouse mirrors God's unconditional love and grace. It sets an example of Christ-like behavior and spiritual maturity. **"Be kind and compassionate to one another, forgiving each other, just as in Christ God forgave you." - Ephesians 4:32.** Forgiveness reflects the grace we receive from God, and those couples who develop the culture of forgiveness within their marriage are distinguished for His continuous uncommon favor.

THE PROCESS OF FORGIVENESS IN MARRIAGE

- **Acknowledging the Hurt**: Recognize and admit the pain caused by your spouse's actions. It is essential to acknowledge your feelings before you can begin the process of forgiveness. **"When I kept silent, my bones wasted away through my groaning all day long." - Psalm 32:3.** Acknowledging pain is the first step towards healing. **" I will speak, that I may be refreshed: I will open my lips and answer."** - Job 32:20

- **Choosing to Forgive**: Forgiveness is a conscious choice, not a feeling. Decide to forgive your spouse, even if the emotions are not immediately aligned with the decision. **"And whenever you stand praying, forgive, if you have anything against anyone, so that your Father also who is in heaven may forgive you your trespasses." - Mark 11:25.** Forgiveness is a decision that aligns with God's will.

- **Communicating Forgiveness**: Let your spouse know that you have forgiven them. This communication can be verbal or through actions that demonstrate forgiveness. **"Therefore, confess your sins to each other and pray for each other so that you may be healed. The prayer of a righteous person is powerful and effective." - James 5:16.** Open communication about forgiveness fosters healing.

- **Letting Go of Resentment**: Release any lingering resentment or desire for revenge. Holding onto negative feelings will hinder the forgiveness process. **"Do not seek revenge or bear a grudge against anyone among your people, but love your neighbor as yourself. I am the Lord." - Leviticus 19:18.** Letting go of grudges is crucial for true forgiveness.

- **Seeking God's Help**: Pray for God's guidance and strength to forgive. Rely on His grace to help you let go of hurt and embrace forgiveness. Remember always that forgiveness is not in your own ability but in the ability of the Spirit of God **"I can do all this through him who gives me strength." - Philippians 4:13.** God provides the strength needed to forgive.

  2Cor 4:7 (KJV) But we have this treasure in earthen vessels, that the excellency of the power may be of God, and not of us.

CHALLENGES TO FORGIVENESS AND HOW TO OVERCOME THEM

- **Pride and Ego**: Pride can hinder forgiveness by making it difficult to admit mistakes or accept apologies.

  Solution: Cultivate humility and remember that everyone makes mistakes. Reflect on your own need for forgiveness and be willing to extend it to your spouse. **"Pride goes before destruction, a haughty spirit before a fall." - Proverbs 16:18.** Humility is key to overcoming pride.

- **Fear of Repetition**: Fear that the hurtful behavior will be repeated can make forgiveness challenging. **Prov 22:4 By humility [and] the fear of the Lord [are] riches, and honor, and life.**

  Solution: Walk by faith and not by fear, and communicate expectations clearly. Trust that with mutual effort and God's help, positive changes can occur. **"For God has not given us a spirit of fear, but of power and of love and of a sound mind." - 2 Timothy 1:7.** Trust in God's provision and protection.

- **Deep Emotional Wounds**: Some hurts run deep and take time to heal, making immediate forgiveness difficult.

  Solution: Deposit all your deep hurts and old wounds unto the Holy Spirit.
  1Pet 5:7 Casting all your care upon him; for the careth for you.
  Be patient with yourself and your spouse as you work through the healing process. **"He heals the brokenhearted and binds up their wounds." - Psalm 147:3.** Trust in God's healing power.

- **Lack of Apology or Remorse**: It can be difficult to forgive when the offending spouse does not apologize or show remorse.

  Solution: Remember that forgiveness is more about your peace and relationship with God than the other person's actions. Forgive even without an apology for your well-being. **"But I tell you, love your enemies and pray for those who persecute you." - Matthew 5:44.** Forgiveness is a personal choice that reflects your character and faith.

PRACTICAL STEPS FOR CULTIVATING FORGIVENESS

- **Pray Together**: Regular prayer as a couple can help invite God's presence and guidance into your marriage, making forgiveness easier. **"For where two or three gather in my name, there am I with them." - Matthew 18:20.** Praying together brings God's presence into your relationship. Let me strongly warn you to be mindful in order to rebuke the voices of the enemy that suddenly appear to resist either spouse from coming together to pray. The devil is greatly aware of the power of agreement between a husband and his wife, the question will always be, do they know?

- **Practice Daily Forgiveness**: Make forgiveness a daily habit. Address minor offenses quickly to prevent them from building up into bigger issues. **"And forgive us our debts, as we also have forgiven our debtors." - Matthew 6:12.** Daily forgiveness reflects God's continuous forgiveness towards us.

- **Seek Counseling**: If forgiveness is particularly challenging, consider seeking help from a marriage counselor or spiritual advisor. **"Where there is no guidance, a people fall, but in an abundance of counselors there is safety." - Proverbs 11:14.** A spiritually mature marriage counselor or coach can provide valuable support.

- **Reflect on God's Forgiveness**: Regularly meditate on the forgiveness you have received from God. This reflection can inspire you to extend the same grace to your spouse. **"Be kind and compassionate to one another, forgiving each other, just as in Christ God forgave you." - Ephesians 4:32.** God's forgiveness is the ultimate model for us to follow.

Forgiveness is a vital element of a healthy and thriving marriage. By embracing forgiveness, couples can overcome conflicts, heal emotional wounds, and build a relationship that reflects God's love and grace.

Resolving Conflicts Biblically

Resolving conflicts biblically is an essential component of maintaining a healthy and thriving marriage. Conflicts are inevitable in any relationship, but how they are handled can either strengthen or weaken the bond between spouses. By applying biblical principles, couples can navigate disagreements in a way that honors God and fosters unity.

UNDERSTANDING CONFLICT IN MARRIAGE

Conflict arises from differences in opinions, desires, and expectations. While these differences are natural, the way they are addressed determines the health of the relationship. The Bible provides guidance on how to manage and resolve conflicts constructively. **James 4:1-2: "What causes fights and quarrels among you? Don't they come from your desires that battle within you? You desire but do not have, so you kill. You covet but you cannot get what you want, so you quarrel and fight. You do not have it because you do not ask God."**

BIBLICAL PRINCIPLES FOR RESOLVING CONFLICTS

- **Seek Peace and Pursue It:** The Bible emphasizes the importance of seeking peace and actively working to maintain it. **Pss 34:14 Depart from evil, and do good; seek peace, and pursue it.**

- This means that couples should strive to create an environment where peace is the goal, rather than winning an argument or proving a point. **Romans 12:18: "If it is possible, as far as it depends on you, live at peace with everyone."**

- **Approach with Humility and Gentleness:** Humility and gentleness are key attitudes when resolving conflicts. Approaching your spouse with a gentle and humble heart can defuse tension and open the door for constructive dialogue. **Ephesians 4:2: "Be completely humble and gentle; be patient, bearing with one another in love."**

- **Speak the Truth in Love:** Honesty is crucial in resolving conflicts, but it must be balanced with love. Speaking the truth in love means expressing your thoughts and feelings honestly while considering the impact of your words on your spouse. **Ephesians 4:15: "Instead, speaking the truth in love, we will grow to become in every respect the mature body of him who is the head, that is, Christ."**

- **Be Quick to Listen, Slow to Speak, and Slow to Anger:** Effective conflict resolution requires good listening skills. By listening carefully and thoughtfully, you show respect and understanding to your spouse. It also helps prevent misunderstandings and unnecessary escalation of conflict. **James 1:19: "My dear brothers and sisters, take note of this: Everyone should be quick to listen, slow to speak and slow to become angry."**

- **Forgive as Christ Forgave:** Forgiveness is a cornerstone of Christian relationships. Holding on to grudges and past hurts can poison a marriage. By forgiving each other, couples can move forward and rebuild trust. **Colossians 3:13: "Bear with each other and forgive one another if any of you has a grievance against someone. Forgive as the Lord forgave you."**

PRACTICAL STEPS FOR BIBLICAL CONFLICT RESOLUTION

- **Pray Together:** Before discussing a conflict, take time to pray together. Ask God for wisdom, patience, and understanding. Prayer invites God's presence into the situation and can help soften hearts. **Philippians 4:6-7: "Do not be anxious about anything, but in every situation, by prayer and petition, with thanksgiving, present your requests to God. And the peace of God, which transcends all understanding, will guard your hearts and your minds in Christ Jesus."**

  Lk 11:2 (KJV) And he said unto them, when ye pray, say, Our Father which art in heaven, Hallowed be thy name. Thy kingdom comes. Thy will be done, as in heaven, so on earth.

- **Define the Issue Clearly:** Both spouses should clearly define the issue at hand. This involves discussing the specific behavior or situation causing the conflict without attacking each other's character. **Proverbs 15:1: "A gentle answer turns away wrath, but a harsh word stirs up anger."**

- **Use "I" Statements:** Communicate your feelings and needs using "I" statements instead of ""your" statements. This reduces the likelihood of your spouse feeling blamed or attacked. Example: "I feel hurt when you don't listen to me" instead of "You never listen to me."

- **Find Common Ground:** Identify areas of agreement and build on them. Finding common ground can help reduce tension and create a sense of partnership in resolving the conflict. **Amos 3:3: "Do two walks together unless they have agreed to do so?"**

- **Seek Wise Counsel:** If a conflict cannot be resolved between the two of you, consider seeking help from a trusted third party, such as a pastor, counselor, or mature Christian couple. **Proverbs 11:14: "Where there is no guidance, a people fall, but in an abundance of counselors there is safety."**

- **Commit to Growth and Change:** Both spouses should be willing to make necessary changes and grow from the experience. This might involve making personal adjustments, improving communication skills, or seeking ongoing support. **Philippians 3:13-14:**

"Brothers and sisters, I do not consider myself yet to have taken hold of it. But one thing I do: Forgetting what is behind and straining toward what is ahead, I press on toward the goal to win the prize for which God has called me heavenward in Christ Jesus."
Isa 43:18 Remember ye not the former things, neither consider the things of old.

THE ROLE OF LOVE IN CONFLICT RESOLUTION

Above all, love should be the guiding principle in resolving conflicts. Love seeks the best for the other person, even in the midst of disagreements. **1 Corinthians 13:4-7: "Love is patient, love is kind. It does not envy, it does not boast, it is not proud. It does not dishonor others, it is not self-seeking, it is not easily angered, it keeps no record of wrongs. Love does not delight in evil but rejoices with the truth. It always protects, always trusts, always hopes, always perseveres."**

By embracing these biblical principles and practical steps, couples can navigate conflicts in a way that strengthens their marriage and brings glory to God. Remember, the goal is not to avoid conflicts altogether but to handle them in a way that fosters growth, understanding, and deeper love for each other.

Qualities of a Godly Couple

QUALITIES OF A HUSBAND

- **Love Sacrificially**: Ephesians 5:25: "Husbands, love your wives, just as Christ also loved the church and gave Himself for her."

  1 Corinthians 13:4-7: "Love is patient, love is kind. It does not envy, it does not boast, it is not proud..."

- **Leads with Humility**: Ephesians 5:23: "For the husband is the head of the wife, as Christ also is the head of the church..."

  Proverbs 4:23: "Keep thy heart with all diligence; for out of it are the issues of life."

- **Protects and Provides**: 1 Timothy 5:8: "But if anyone does not provide for his own, and especially for those of his household, he has denied the faith and is worse than an unbeliever."

  Ephesians 5:28-29: "So ought men to love their wives as their own bodies. He that loveth his wife loveth himself. For no man ever yet hated his own flesh; but nourisheth and cherisheth it, even as the Lord the church."

- **Exercises Self-Control**: 1 Corinthians 9:27: "But I discipline my body and keep it under control, lest after preaching to others I myself should be disqualified."

  Proverbs 25:28: "Like a city whose walls are broken through is a person who lacks self-control."

- **Cultivates Spiritual Growth**: 1 Peter 3:7: "Husbands, likewise, dwell with them with understanding, giving honor to the wife, as to the weaker vessel, and as being heirs together of the grace of life, that your prayers may not be hindered."

  John 17:17: "Sanctify them by Your truth. Your word is the truth."

  Gen 2:8 And the Lord God planted a garden eastward in Eden; and there he put the man whom he had formed.

- **Exemplifies Integrity**: Proverbs 20:7: "The righteous man walks in his integrity; His children are blessed after him."

  Job 2:10: "But he said to her, 'You speak as one of the foolish women speaks. Shall we indeed accept good from God, and shall we not accept adversity?' In all this Job did not sin with his lips."

- **Supports and Encourages**: 1 Thessalonians 5:11: "Therefore comfort each other and edify one another, just as you also are doing."

  Proverbs 12:25: "Anxiety in the heart of man causes depression, but a good word makes it glad."

  Eph 5:28 So ought men to love their wives as their own bodies. He that loveth his wife loveth himself.

- **Visionary**: Prov 29:18 Where [there is] no vision, the people perish: but he that keepeth the law, happy [is] he.
- **Takes Accountability**: Genesis 3:12 And the man said, the woman whom thou gavest [to be] with me, she gave me of the tree, and I did eat.

- **Invest Time in teaching His household God's Word**: Gen 18:19 For I know him, that he will command his children and his household after him, and they shall keep the way of the Lord, to do justice and judgment; that the Lord may bring upon Abraham that which he hath spoken of him.

- **Make use of time**: Ephesians 5:16 Redeeming the time, because the days are evil.

- **Disciplines his eyes**: Job 31:1 I made a covenant with my eyes; why then should I think upon a maid?

  Prov 27:20 Hell and destruction are never full; so, the eyes of man are never satisfied.

  Psalms 25:15 Mine eyes [are] ever toward the Lord; for he shall pluck my feet out of the net.

  - Does not physically harm his wife.

  Eph 5:28 So ought men to love their wives as their own bodies. He that loveth his wife loveth himself.

QUALITIES OF GODLY A WIFE

- **Respects Her Husband**: Ephesians 5:33: "Nevertheless let each one of you in particular so love his own wife as himself, and let the wife see that she respects her husband."

  1 Peter 3:1-2: "Wives, likewise, be submissive to your own husbands, that even if some do not obey the word, they, without a word, may be won by the conduct of their wives, when they observe your chaste conduct accompanied by fear."

- **Cultivates a Gentle and Quiet Spirit**: 1 Peter 3:4: "Rather, it should be that of your inner self, the unfading beauty of a gentle and quiet spirit, which is of great worth in God's sight."

  Proverbs 31:26: "She opens her mouth with wisdom, and on her tongue is the law of kindness."

- **Demonstrates Wisdom and Discretion**: Proverbs 31:26: "She opens her mouth with wisdom, and on her tongue is the law of kindness."

  Proverbs 14:1: "The wise woman builds her house, but with her own hands the foolish one tears hers down."

  Prov 19:14 House and riches [are] the inheritance of fathers: and a prudent wife [is] from the Lord.

  2Kgs 4:9 And she said unto her husband, behold now, I perceive that this [is] an holy man of God, which passeth by us continually.

- **Shows Compassion and Kindness**: Proverbs 31:20: "She extends her hand to the poor, yes, she reaches out her hands to the needy."

  Ephesians 4:32: "And be kind to one another, tenderhearted, forgiving one another, even as God in Christ forgave you."

- **Exemplifies Purity and Holiness**: Titus 2:3-5: "The older women likewise, that they be reverent in behavior, not slanderers, not given to much wine, teachers of good things—that they admonish the young women to love their husbands, to love their children, to be discreet, chaste, homemakers, good, obedient to their own husbands, that the word of God may not be blasphemed."

  1 Timothy 2:9-10: "In like manner also, that the women adorn themselves in modest apparel, with propriety and moderation, not with braided hair or gold or pearls or costly clothing, but which is proper for women professing godliness, with good works."

- **Supports and Encourages**: Proverbs 31:11-12: "The heart of her husband safely trusts her; so, he will have no lack of gain. She does him good and not evil all the days of her life."

  1 Thessalonians 5:11: "Therefore comfort each other and edify one another, just as you also are doing."

  Ruth 1:16 And Ruth said, Intreat me not to leave thee, [or] to return from following after thee: for whither thou goest, I will go; and where thou lodgest, I will lodge: thy people [shall be] my people, and thy God my God:

- **Exercises Self-Control**: Proverbs 31:27: "She watches over the ways of her household, and does not eat the bread of idleness."

  1 Timothy 2:9-10: "In like manner also, that the women adorn themselves in modest apparel, with propriety and moderation, not with braided hair or gold or pearls or costly clothing, but which is proper for women professing godliness, with good works."

  reflecting the godly qualities that contribute to a harmonious and spiritually enriched marriage.

- **Lives a life of subjection unto her husband**: Gen 24:65 For she [had] said unto the servant, What man [is] this that walketh in the field to meet us? And the servant [had] said, It [is] my master: therefore she took a vail, and covered herself.
- **Selfless Laborer**: Gen 24:19 And when she had finished giving him drink, she said, I will draw [water] for thy camels also, until they have done drinking.

  Gen 24:20 And she hasted, and emptied her pitcher into the trough, and ran again unto the well to draw [water], and drew for all his camels.

- **Detailed in her services towards the Lord**: 2Kgs 4:10 Let us make a little chamber, I pray thee, on the wall; and let us set for him there a bed, and a table, and a stool, and a candlestick: and it shall be, when he cometh to us, that he shall turn in thither.
- **Makes room for God's anointing to flow into her home**: 2Kgs 4:8 And it fell on a day, that Elisha passed to Shunem, where [was] a great woman; and she constrained him to eat bread. And [so] it was, [that] as oft as he passed by, he turned in thither to eat bread.

  2Kgs 4:9 And she said unto her husband, behold now, I perceive that this [is] an holy man of God, which passeth by us continually.

  2Kgs 4:10 Let us make a little chamber, I pray thee, on the wall; and let us set for him there a bed, and a table, and a stool, and a candlestick: and it shall be, when he cometh to us, that he shall turn in thither.

- **Does not taunt or provoke her husband**: Prov 25:24 It is better to be living in an angle of the house-top, than with a bitter-tongued woman in a wide house.

- Spiritual Force against the enemy.

Esther 4:16 Go, gather together all the Jews that are present in Shushan, and fast ye for me, and neither eat nor drink three days, night or day: I also and my maidens will fast likewise; and so, will I go in unto the king, which [is] not according to the law: and if I perish, I perish.

CHAPTER 4

LOVE, RESPECT, AND INTIMACY

UNDERSTANDING THE BIBLICAL CONCEPT OF LOVE

Chapter Four
Love, Respect, and Intimacy
Understanding the Biblical Concept of Love

DEFINITION OF LOVE

In the biblical context, love transcends mere emotions and physical attraction. It is an act of the will, a commitment to act in the best interest of another person. Biblical love, especially in marriage, is selfless, sacrificial, and unconditional, mirroring the love that Christ has for His church.

Agape/Sacrificial Love: Agape love also called sacrificial love is the highest form of love, which is selfless, sacrificial, and unconditional. This type of love is characterized by a commitment to the well-being of the spouse, regardless of circumstances. It is the love that Jesus Christ demonstrated through His life and death. **Roman 5:8 But God has made clear his love to us, in that, when we were still sinners, Christ gave his life for us.**

God's Basis for Love in Marriage: Ephesians 5:25-28: **"Husbands, love your wives, just as Christ loved the church and gave himself up for her to make her holy, cleansing her by the washing with water through the word, and to present her to himself as a radiant church, without stain or wrinkle or any other blemish, but holy and blameless. In this same way, husbands ought to love their wives as their own bodies. He who loves his wife loves himself."** This passage emphasizes that the husband's love for his wife should reflect Christ's sacrificial love for the church. It involves a commitment to nurture, protect, and cherish her.

1 Corinthians 13:4-7: "Love is patient, love is kind. It does not envy, it does not boast, it is not proud. It does not dishonor others, it is not self-seeking, it is not easily angered, it keeps no record of wrongs. Love does not delight in evil but rejoices with the truth. It always protects, always trusts, always hopes, always perseveres." These verses provide a comprehensive description of love's attributes. In marriage, these qualities should be evident in the daily interactions between spouses.

PRACTICAL APPLICATIONS OF BIBLICAL LOVE IN MARRIAGE

- **Sacrificial Love:** Husbands are called to love their wives sacrificially, as Christ loved the church. This means putting her needs above his own, being willing to make sacrifices for her well-being, and continually seeking her good.

- **Unconditional Love:** Agape Love in marriage should not be based on conditions or reciprocation. It is a commitment to love your spouse regardless of their actions or circumstances, reflecting the unconditional love of God.

- **Daily Acts of Kindness:** Demonstrating love through small, daily acts of kindness and consideration. This can include helping with household chores, offering words of encouragement, and being attentive to your spouse's needs and feelings.

- **Forgiveness:** Agape Love keeps no record of wrongs. In marriage, this means being willing to forgive your spouse's mistakes and not holding grudges. Forgiveness is essential for maintaining a healthy and loving relationship.

THE ROLE OF LOVE IN STRENGTHENING THE MARITAL BOND

- **Emotional Connection:** Agape Love fosters a deep emotional connection between spouses. It creates a safe environment where both partners can be vulnerable, express their feelings, and support each other.

- **Spiritual Growth:** A loving relationship encourages spiritual growth. When both spouses love each other with the love of Christ, they help each other grow in faith and draw closer to God to impact their community.

- **Conflict Resolution:** Agape Love plays a crucial role in resolving conflicts. When spouses love each other, they are more likely to approach disagreements with a desire to understand, reconcile, and maintain harmony in the relationship.

- **Building Trust:** Consistent expressions of love build trust in the marriage. Trust is foundational for a strong and healthy relationship, and it grows when both partners feel loved and valued.

- Understanding and practicing biblical love is essential for a thriving marriage. It requires a commitment to selflessness, sacrifice, and unconditional love, reflecting the love that Christ has for His church. By applying the principles of biblical love, couples can strengthen their emotional and spiritual bond, resolve conflicts effectively, and build a marriage that honors God.

The Role of Respect in a Healthy Marriage
DEFINITION OF RESPECT

Respect in marriage involves recognizing and appreciating the value of your spouse. It means treating your partner with dignity, honoring their thoughts and feelings, and showing consideration for their needs and desires. Respect is a crucial component of love and is essential for a healthy, thriving marriage.

FOUNDATION FOR RESPECT IN MARRIAGE

- **Ephesians 5:33: "However, each one of you also must love his wife as he loves himself, and the wife must respect her husband."** This verse highlights the dual roles in marriage: husbands are to love their wives, and wives are to respect their husbands. Respect is seen as a foundational element that complements love.

- **1 Peter 3:7: "Husbands, in the same way be considerate as you live with your wives, and treat them with respect as the weaker partner and as heirs with you of the gracious gift of life, so that nothing will hinder your prayers." Husbands are called to respect their wives, acknowledging their shared inheritance in the grace of life. This mutual respect is essential for spiritual harmony and effective prayer.

PRACTICAL APPLICATIONS OF RESPECT IN MARRIAGE

- **Listening Attentively:** Respect is demonstrated by actively listening to your spouse. This involves giving them your full attention, acknowledging their viewpoints, and showing empathy towards their concerns.
- **Valuing Opinions:** Respecting your spouse means valuing their opinions and considering their perspective when making decisions. This fosters a sense of partnership and mutual understanding in the relationship.
- **Speaking Kindly:** Respectful communication involves speaking kindly and avoiding harsh or critical language. It's important to build up your spouse with words of affirmation and encouragement.
- **Appreciating Contributions:** Acknowledge and appreciate your spouse's contributions to the marriage and family. This can include expressing gratitude for their efforts, recognizing their hard work, and celebrating their achievements.
- **Honoring Boundaries:** Respect includes honoring your spouse's boundaries and personal space. This means being considerate of their need for privacy, rest, and individual time.
- **Supporting Growth:** Encourage and support your spouse's personal and professional growth. Show interest in their goals and aspirations, and provide the necessary support for them to succeed.

THE IMPACT OF RESPECT ON MARITAL HEALTH

- **Strengthening Trust:** Respect builds trust in the marriage. When spouses feel respected, they are more likely to trust each other, leading to a deeper and more secure relationship.
- **Enhancing Communication:** Respectful communication fosters open and honest dialogue. When both partners feel heard and valued, they are more willing to share their thoughts and feelings, which enhances understanding and intimacy.
- **Reducing Conflicts:** Respect helps in managing and reducing conflicts. When spouses approach disagreements with a respectful attitude, they are more likely to find amicable solutions and maintain harmony in the relationship.
- **Promoting Emotional Security:** Feeling respected contributes to emotional security. When spouses know they are valued and appreciated, they feel more confident and secure in their relationship.
- **Encouraging Mutual Growth:** Respect encourages mutual growth and development. Spouses who respect each other are more likely to support and motivate each other to reach their full potential.

- **Respect and Submission in Marriage:** The concept of respect in marriage is often linked to the idea of submission, particularly in the biblical context. It is important to understand that submission is not about inferiority or domination but about mutual respect and love.

  Ephesians 5:21: "Submit to one another out of reverence for Christ." This verse emphasizes mutual submission, where both spouses are called to respect and honor each other out of reverence for Christ.

  Ephesians 5:22-24: "Wives, submit yourselves to your own husbands as you do to the Lord. For the husband is the head of the wife as Christ is the head of the church, his body, of which he is the Savior. Now as the church submits to Christ, so also wives should submit to their husbands in everything." Submission in this context is about respecting the husband's role as the head of the household, while the husband is called to love his wife sacrificially.

  Ephesians 5:25-28: "Husbands, love your wives, just as Christ loved the church and gave himself up for her... In this same way, husband's ought to love their wives as their own bodies. He who loves his wife loves himself." Husbands are to love their wives with a self-sacrificial love that fosters respect and unity in the marriage.

CULTIVATING A CULTURE OF RESPECT IN MARRIAGE

- **Lead by Example:** Both spouses should lead by example in showing respect. Demonstrating respect in your actions and words sets a positive tone for the relationship.

- **Practice Gratitude:** Regularly express gratitude for your spouse and their contributions. This reinforces their sense of value and fosters a culture of appreciation.

- **Prioritize Communication:** Make communication a priority. Regularly check in with each other, discuss important matters, and address any issues respectfully and constructively.

- **Seek Understanding:** Strive to understand your spouse's perspective, needs, and feelings. This helps in building empathy and fostering a deeper connection.

- **Forgive and Move Forward:** Practice forgiveness and let go of past grievances. Holding onto resentment can erode respect and trust in the marriage.

Respect is a fundamental element of a healthy marriage. It involves valuing and honoring your spouse, treating them with kindness and consideration, and fostering an environment of mutual appreciation and support. By cultivating respect, couples can strengthen their emotional and spiritual bond, enhance communication, and create a loving and harmonious relationship that honors God's design for marriage.

God's Design for Marital Intimacy
DEFINITION AND IMPORTANCE OF MARITAL INTIMACY

Marital intimacy is the deep, personal connection between a husband and wife that encompasses physical, emotional, and spiritual closeness. It is a vital component of a healthy marriage, fostering a sense of unity, trust, and mutual satisfaction. God's design for marital intimacy is rooted in love, respect, and commitment, creating a bond that reflects His relationship with the Church.

FOUNDATION FOR MARITAL INTIMACY

- **Genesis 2:24: "Therefore a man shall leave his father and mother and be joined to his wife, and they shall become one flesh."** This verse underscores the divine intention for marital intimacy, emphasizing the physical and spiritual union of husband and wife. The "one flesh" relationship signifies the profound connection and unity that is exclusive to marriage.

- **Proverbs 5:18-19: "Let your fountain be blessed, and rejoice in the wife of your youth. A loving doe, a graceful deer—may her breasts satisfy you always, may you ever be intoxicated with her love."** This passage celebrates the joy and pleasure of marital intimacy, encouraging spouses to find delight and fulfillment in each other.

- **1 Corinthians 7:3-5: "The husband should fulfill his marital duty to his wife, and likewise the wife to her husband. The wife does not have authority over her own body but yields it to her husband. In the same way, the husband does not have authority over his own body but yields it to his wife. Do not deprive each other except perhaps by mutual consent and for a time, so that you may devote yourselves to prayer. Then come together again so that Satan will not tempt you because of your lack of self-control."** This passage highlights the mutual responsibilities of husbands and wives to satisfy each other's sexual needs, emphasizing the importance of regular, consensual intimacy to maintain a strong marital bond and prevent temptation.

COMPONENTS OF MARITAL INTIMACY

- **Physical Intimacy:** Physical intimacy involves sexual relations, affection, and touch. It is a vital expression of love and desire, fostering a deep connection between spouses. Healthy physical intimacy requires mutual consent, respect, and communication to ensure both partners feel valued and satisfied.

- **Emotional Intimacy:** Emotional intimacy is the closeness and vulnerability shared between spouses. It involves open communication, sharing feelings, and providing emotional support. Building emotional intimacy requires trust, empathy, and a commitment to understanding and meeting each other's emotional needs.

- **Spiritual Intimacy:** Spiritual intimacy is the shared faith and spiritual practices that unite a couple. Praying together, studying the Bible, and participating in worship and service strengthen the spiritual bond between spouses. Spiritual intimacy fosters a sense of purpose and direction, aligning the couple's values and goals with God's will.

GOD'S DESIGN FOR MARITAL INTIMACY

- **Unity and Oneness:** God's design for marital intimacy is rooted in the concept of oneness. This unity is not only physical but also emotional and spiritual. The intimate relationship between husband and wife mirrors the unity of the Father, Son, and the Holy Spirit and the relationship between Christ and His Church.

- **Mutual Pleasure and Satisfaction:** Marital intimacy is meant to be a source of mutual pleasure and satisfaction. God created sex to be enjoyed within the confines of marriage, providing a means for spouses to express love, passion, and desire. This mutual enjoyment strengthens the marital bond and fosters a deeper connection.

- **Procreation and Partnership:** One of the purposes of marital intimacy is procreation. Through sexual union, couples participate in God's creative work, bringing new life into the world. Beyond procreation, intimacy fosters partnership, helping spouses to grow together and support each other in their journey of faith and life.

- **Protection Against Temptation:** Regular, satisfying marital intimacy serves as a safeguard against sexual temptation. By fulfilling each other's needs and desires, spouses reduce the risk of infidelity and maintain a strong, exclusive bond.

PRACTICAL STEPS TO FOSTER MARITAL INTIMACY

- **Prioritize Time Together:** Make intentional efforts to spend quality time together. Regular date nights, shared activities, and intimate moments help to strengthen the bond and keep the relationship vibrant.

- **Communicate Openly and Honestly:** Effective communication is crucial for intimacy. Discuss your needs, desires, and concerns openly and honestly. Listen to each other with empathy and understanding, and address any issues promptly and respectfully.

- **Show Affection and Appreciation:** Express love and appreciation through words and actions. Regularly show affection through touch, hugs, kisses, and kind gestures. Appreciation and affirmation foster a positive atmosphere and strengthen the emotional connection.

- **Maintain Physical Health and Well-being:** Physical health impacts intimacy. Take care of your bodies through proper nutrition, exercise, and rest. Address any medical issues that may affect sexual intimacy and seek professional help if needed.

- **Cultivate Spiritual Growth:** Grow together spiritually by praying, studying the Bible, and attending church together. Engage in spiritual practices that deepen your faith and enhance your spiritual intimacy.

- **Seek Professional Help if Needed:** If you face challenges in your marital intimacy, do not hesitate to seek professional help. Marriage counseling, therapy, or guidance from a trusted spiritual advisor can provide valuable support and solutions.

God's design for marital intimacy is a beautiful and integral part of marriage. It involves a harmonious blend of physical, emotional, and spiritual connections that reflect the unity and love between Christ and the Church. By understanding and embracing this divine design, couples can foster a deep, fulfilling, and lasting bond that honors God and brings joy and fulfillment to their relationship.

The Battle of Rulership

The Holy Spirit has impressed upon my heart the necessity of expressing to all women the knowledge and understanding of their true identity.

Genesis 2:23 says, "And Adam said, this is now bone of my bones, and flesh of my flesh: she shall be called Woman, because she was taken out of Man." This scripture underscores your identity, rooted in the divine blueprint of your Creator.

It is crucial to dismantle any falsehoods you may have internalized before entering the sacred covenant of marriage. As a wife and woman, you are the Creator's secret weapon, designed with unique capabilities to fulfill a divine purpose.

In the Garden of Eden, your God-given managerial abilities were essential, and they remain vital in every husband's life today. Your role as a helpmate is integral to the fulfillment of the kingdom's purpose within your marriage.

To succeed gracefully in this divine role, you must submit to the position that has been bestowed upon you by your Maker. What I am about to share with you is invaluable wisdom from the mind of God that will significantly contribute to the success of your marriage.

If you desire the Holy Spirit to govern your marriage, you must first embrace your divine position.

After the fall of man, meaning when the sin of Adam and Eve, our Heavenly Father took steps to ensure His plans would not be thwarted again. One of these steps was to guarantee that women would be free and protected to express all the blessedness He has placed within them.

Genesis 3:16 declares, "Unto the woman he said, I will greatly multiply thy sorrow and thy conception; in sorrow thou shalt bring forth children; and thy desire shall be to thy husband, and he shall rule over there."

WHAT DO I MEAN BY DIVINE POSITION?

After the serpent deceived Eve to help her husband Adam disobey God's instruction in the garden, there were consequences that were given by God Our Father to all parties who contributed to such disobedience. Based on what Eve did in the garden when she took it upon herself to assume the position of authority over her husband Adam, she was given the role that will better assist her in achieving true beauty and success in life.

Therefore the only way the wife/woman can achieve her role in marriage as the helpmate is for her to discover, and submit to God's original position for her life in **Gen 3:16. "Wives/women, maybe people around you are afraid to tell you this truth, but by the Spirit of God in me, I say to your spirit that you are not the head or authority in God's institution of marriage, it is your husband whether he knows it or not. I know many days, you might feel tempted to play the role of the head due to the spiritual condition of your husband/man, or society's pressure, or the voice of the devil in your ears, I want to encourage you by saying to you that this position as the head in God's organization was never bestowed upon you by your Maker/Manufacturer."**

God who made you, knows everything about you, He knows your weaknesses as well as your strength. God who made you knows truly well the qualities in you that define your true beauty for His glory and kingdom advancement.

God placed you in a position where you can be more effective concerning His will for His human family. Let me first inform you that the woman/wife has always been God's secret weapon, but only if they are willing to discover their true place of authority, which is to submit, or to be in submission to His designated position.

YOU ASK WHAT IS THIS POSITION?

Allow me to explain! After the enemy came into the garden and deceived the woman, God placed the woman into a position of subjection, or submissiveness not to belittle or diminish her but only to set her up for greater works in His marriage institution.

Gen 3:6 And when the woman saw that the tree [was] good for food, and that it [was] pleasant to the eyes, and a tree to be desired to make [one] wise, she took of the fruit thereof, and did eat, and gave also unto her husband with her; and he did eat.

I want every woman to hear me well through the influence of the Holy Spirit when I say that Lord Jesus understands very well that life has been harsh on every woman since the fall, and especially with men who are supposed to assist the woman by being in their role, but are yet suffering from an identity crisis themselves. Society has also contributed to the woman's disorder by redefining the woman's divine role; past relationships have reshaped the mindset of our women to focus more on fighting for their equal rights instead of God's truth. Nevertheless, it's never too late when King Jesus is alive and on His throne. In order to be a victorious kingdom woman/wife, every woman must submit to God's position for their life as His product.

1Pet 3:1 "Likewise, ye wives, [be] in subjection to your own husbands; that, if any obey not the word, they also may without the word be won by the conversation of the wives;"

What does it mean to be in subjection? Is this an expression of weakness or insult towards the woman? In no way possible can the word of God instruct anything that is not for the purpose of the advancement of one's life.

Here is the Greek definition for this word be in subjection:

HUPOTASSŌ)

- To arrange under, to subordinate
- To subject, put in subjection
- To subject oneself, obey
- To submit to one's control
- To yield to one's admonition or advice
- To obey, be subject

As the Wife/woman, you were made to be a solution, and not a pollution on earth or in your marriage relationships. You are God's incubator in His human family for His kingdom advancement on earth.

So many women today are struggling to accept this truth of God's law, and what's worse is that they are being cheered on by the same serpent from the garden who has systematically deceived women in this generation by administering his lies into their minds at his various institutions within the society.

The Women of today are now crowning themselves as the head in their marriages, referring to themselves as Apostles, Archbishops, Senior Pastors of the Lord's church. This desire to have authority is nothing new, and are all indicators of their ignorance of God's purpose for their lives. So often I would have to rebuke so called men of God who tolerate such disorder in the body of Christ under their watch. We must stand firm in our generation to protect our beautiful women from the temptation of that same old crooked serpent who enticed Eve to walk opposite of the will of God in the garden. Let there be order in our marriages, and in the house of God, it is the truth that makes us free.

1Cor 14:40 "Let all things be done in the right and ordered way"

In Today's society, women are driven to find their own husbands/men, women are proudly proclaiming themselves as independent, women are transforming themselves into more masculinity appearance, women are driven to position themselves in the places of authority for the sole purpose of rubbing shoulders with the man who was created in the image and likeness of the Creator.

1Cor 11:7 For a man indeed ought not to cover [his] head, forasmuch as he is the image and glory of God: but the woman is the glory of the man.

Women today are being approached and deceived by that same serpent from the garden who teaches them to be full of pride, and rebellious. This is an attack against the divine order of the Creator for His kingdom advancement through the human family. The same enemy who caused the confusion in the garden is diligently at work in our generation.

The unfortunate reality is that these same women who have been deceived by such ungodly ideologies, full of pride, and hungry for power are the same ones entering into marriages hoping to achieve in an institution that requires the exact opposite of the negative mindset they have adopted from the devil.

When I met my wife Victorious, she was a prime example of a so-called independent woman, a precious and gifted woman who was ignorant to her divine position.

WHERE DOES THIS ATTITUDE DIMINISHING OUR WOMEN TODAY COME FROM?

This mindset that has been developed in the women today was inherited from their mother Eve, the first woman from the garden. God ultimately did not blame Eve but the reality is that Eve had no business whatsoever to act on her own when the serpent approached her to tempt her. Though our women today will justify the pride of Eve by questioning the whereabouts of her husband Adam, and his inability to relate what God instructed him to his wife. I want to put this unbiblical justification to rest by pointing out that Adam did in fact relate to His wife Eve what God instructed Him not to do. How do we know if Adam instructed Eve?

We can conclude that Eve had the information from her husband by her response to the serpent.

Gen 3:2 And the woman said unto the serpent, we may eat of the fruit of the trees of the garden:

Gen 3:3 But of the fruit of the tree which [is] in the midst of the garden, God hath said, Ye shall not eat of it, neither shall ye touch it, lest ye die.

Eve's crime was not the fact that she was approached by the serpent but that she refused to consult her head when she was approached by the serpent. This is exactly what the serpent is after in all marriages, a woman who is eager to usurp authority over her husband by breaking divine order.

1Cor 11:3 But I would have you know, that the head of every man is Christ; and the head of the woman [is] the man; and the head of Christ [is] God.

THERE IS NOTHING NEW UNDER THE SUN!

I thank God that He blessed Victorious with a true man of God (myself) who was not perfect by no means but was endowed with the fear of the Lord, and His word.

After my wife and I got married, attempting to teach her to walk in subjection towards me, her head was a very strange thing for her. Even when I attempted to correct her by presenting some Bible verses to her as evidence to mend her ways, she would reject me rebelliously. I could not blame her because at the time no one had taught her that such behaviors being portrayed by her were inherited attitudes from her mother Eve, "the apple doesn't fall far from the tree."

1Tim 2:14 And Adam was not deceived, but the woman being deceived was in the transgression. Women/Wives, I want to let you know that the Lord totally understands your current state. My wife Victorious was once a rebellious woman, maybe even worse in some cases, but I have seen the Holy Spirit change this once angry, and disobedient wife of mine into a humble submissive soul right before my eyes. Now her transformation was not easy, it took prayer, faith mixed with work to arrive at this glorious result.

Jas 2:26 (KJV) For as the body without the spirit is dead, so faith without works is dead also.

What I am saying to you is that there is hope, you can make the change today to live according to God's design position for your life, wife/woman. Every future successful story is based on a woman/Wives discovering God's designed position for them.

One of the biggest mistakes that most wives/women make in their marriages and relationships is when they come into it with the mindset that God has chosen them to change their husbands/men by trying to rule over them.

This method will not only fail but will be received by the husband/man as a clear disrespect. I promise you ladies that no man wakes up in the morning and prays for the Lord to send them a loud and disrespectful woman who has no conviction of God's divine order for her life. My wife definitely used this unruly method as a means to solve many of our marital issues. Yes! She was the type of wife/woman that was accustomed to talking a lot without taking a moment to pray. When Victorious and I first got married she had an aggressive behavior. If you can relate to this, then you can agree that indeed the Holy Spirit is speaking to you to start working on being quieter and gentler in your marriage/relationship. **Prov 25:24 [It is] better to dwell in the corner of the housetop, than with a brawling woman and in a wide house.**

It's amazing what the devil and his deceptive teaching have turned our women into in this generation. I have seen women completely dismantle their husbands with the most degrading words only to meet them later for a round of make-up sex! Lord has mercy! The woman was not designed and called to the ministry of loudness, and foolishness.

Prov 9:13 "A foolish woman [is] clamorous: [she is] simple, and knoweth nothing"

Prov 9:13 "The foolish woman is full of noise; she has no sense at all"

1Tim 2:11 "Let the woman learn in silence with all subjection"

Now ladies I say these things only to encourage your spirit to repent, meaning it's time to change your mind for the better in rejection of your past ways, behaviors, attitude, unbiblical doctrines, upbringing. I do also want to stress to you that God your Father is not against the woman's ability to freely express herself or to express her natural leadership qualities. The Lord God, Our Good Father simply does not want the woman to be misinterpreted, or misunderstood due to her ungoverned emotions like what transpired in the garden. Marriage and the human family are the Lord's holy organization, and for any organization to effectively operate, there must be a specified head or leader, and it is not the woman. God loves all women and He intentionally put this boundary in place to protect the woman from every form of attack from the kingdom of darkness. When the woman is in alignment with the spirit of her Maker, she is the most powerful spiritual being on planet earth.

The Lord's desire is for every woman to be in tuned with their spiritual nature, this is the part of them that is beautiful, and supposed to lead every other part of her life.

When a wife/woman is not mature spiritually, the enemy will use her emotions to tarnish God's beauty within her, and ultimately turn her into a destroyer instead of a helpmate, builder, manager.

Prov 14:1 Wisdom is building her house, but the foolish woman is pulling it down with her hands. In today's society, women are more desperate than ever to get married without first attempting to prepare themselves spiritually to endure in their marriages. Women are suffering from an identity crisis just as the men are, and what's worse is that young girls are learning from these same disorderly women/wives.

I once knew an angry, loud mouth, hard heady young lady who had no regards to mature spiritually. This same young lady soon decided to go to Africa to get herself a husband! Well, she got married in Africa and brought her husband back to America to live together. After one month of her arriving with her new husband, I received a phone call from her stating that her husband wanted to divorce her. I asked myself" what would make this man who was so blessed to have a woman travel all the way to Africa to marry him now want to divorce her in less than a year?

I soon received the answer to my question after I spoke with this husband. He informed me that after arriving in the United States with his wife, she had repeatedly disrespected him verbally and physically and constantly reminded him of how useless he is, and that she could make him, or break him! This husband was in tears, and insecure in such a short time of experiencing his wife in America. What happened here? This woman was out of the will of God, out of order, unprepared, prideful, and destructive to herself and everyone else. She thought because she had the ability to financially bring a husband to another country, this would somehow preserve the marriage. I have discovered from this woman's story along with many other women, that they meant well for desiring marriage but their common error is that they were ignorant to God's identity for their lives.

Prov 19:21 A man's heart may be full of designs, but the purpose of the Lord is unchanging.

This story is meant for the purpose of illustrating the reality of how quickly a wife/woman can be used to play the role of a destroying mate instead of a Helpmate.

This is exactly the reality of the problem that exists within our society today, treading across every community globally. Wives/women are victims of mixed Identities that blinds them from discovering their divine identity. Hair and makeup have taken the place of God's standard of the true beauty of the woman.

Prov 31:30 "Favor [is] deceitful, and beauty [is] vain: [but] a woman [that] feareth the Lord, she shall be praised." Every woman married today, single, or heading into the direction of marriage needs to understand that their physical appearance alone cannot not maintain it, nor can they charm their way into achieving the kind of fulfillment that comes from walking in discovering God's identity for them.

True happiness is possible when the wife/woman discovers her divine position, only then will her outward beauty be of any significance.

God created the woman to be a helpmate for the purpose of helping her husband to fulfill the purpose of their Creator.

The way to the man's heart was never through his stomach, or how much sex he is offered daily.

God made the woman and brought her to Adam in the territory where Adam her husband was busy fulfilling His purpose in the garden, God's presence.

1Pet 3:3 "Whose adorning let it not be that outward [adorning] of plaiting the hair, and of wearing of gold, or of putting on of apparel"

Seeing my wife Victorious making the intentional effort to respect, and to honor me today as her husband was a difficult new path for her because the Lord had indeed blessed her with physical beauty!

As my wife started to apply the biblical knowledge of her role, the Holy Spirit began to touch her enabling her to accept and to embrace this new change happening in her heart, and pouring into our marriage.

I started to see my wife who used to be so aggressive towards me during our disagreements, now retreating into her closer to pray instead of standing to exchange words with me! I have to admit this was strange to me being in the same house where I would hear her screaming in prayer unto the Lord to humble her and to raid her of her old self! That alone humbled me to repeat what she was doing! The Lord had taken away my fighting partner, and gave me a prayer partner!

1Pet 3:1 Wives, be ruled by your husbands; so that even if some of them give no attention to the word, their hearts may be changed by the behavior of their wives,

One time, after my wife and I had a very big verbal altercation, she retreated to her prayer closet where I could hear her praying unto the Lord loudly saying "Lord teach me, break me, touch my lips, help me, help my husband."

In my heart as her husband, I was like what is going on? This my wife is being transformed right before my eyes!

It was like the more knowledge my wife acquired about her divine position of subjection, the more she applied them practically, and developed spiritual fruit pleasing unto the Lord.

I believe when a wife/woman does not understand that her humility is her authorized batch that pleases God, she will continue to live only to express counterfeit batches instead.

My wife was maturing spiritually which influenced my life as her husband, Pastor, and father tremendously.

She would address me as her lord just as Sarah would call her husband Abraham in the old time! The scripture was coming alive in my wife's life, she was obeying the word of God and not only being a hearer. In today's generation, if you even mentioned to a woman to refer to their husbands/men as lords, they would all grab some pies to throw in your direction!

I can tell you; Sarah was a wise kingdom woman, she did not refer to Abraham as lord because she was being abused, or in fear of him, this is a relational approach by any woman/wife whom the Spirit of the Lord will touch.

1Pet 3:6 "As Sarah was ruled by Abraham, naming him lord; whose children you are if you do well, and are not put in fear by any danger"

These qualities of a spiritual mature woman are lacking in today's society, and also frowned upon by wives/women who lack the knowledge of its significance.

The word lord means owner, leader, master, chief:

Whoever you refer to as Lord, owns you, therefore Sarah was being a spiritually mature wise woman by letting her husband know that he owns her.

Let me ask you this question, wife/woman, does your husband have this confidence in your level of submission towards him?

Does he truly feel like he is your lord? Do you treat him as your lord?

The reality is many husbands would answer "No" in front of their wives before they can even have the opportunity to respond.

Here is the revelation of expressing true submission to your husband, he has to know that he owns you in order to provide or protect you. The tragedy is that many husbands cannot honestly admit it.

When my wife began to perceive me, her husband as her lord, this act of subjection towards me impacted me spiritually. It awakened something in me that would have never been awakened if she had never obeyed the Holy Spirit to submit to her divine position.

THE DANGERS OF TECHNOLOGY IN MARRIAGE AND FAMILY LIFE

1Cor 6:12 (BBE) I am free to do all things; but not all things are wise. I am free to do all things; but I will not let myself come under the power of any.

In today's digital age, technology has become an integral part of our lives. While it offers many benefits, it also poses significant challenges to marriage and family life, particularly when it comes to communication and intimacy. The overuse of cell phones, tablets, and other devices can create distance between spouses and weaken the bonds that hold a family together.

THE IMPACT ON MARITAL INTIMACY

Technology, when used excessively or inappropriately, can be a barrier to marital intimacy. Couples often find themselves physically present but emotionally distant, as one or both partners are engrossed in their phones or other devices. This distraction can prevent meaningful conversations and reduce the quality of time spent together. Over time, this can lead to a weakening of the emotional connection that is vital for a healthy marriage.

When couples prioritize screen time over face-to-face interaction, they miss out on the opportunity to nurture their relationship. Intimacy is built on communication, both verbal and non-verbal, and when technology intrudes, it diminishes the opportunities for these critical interactions.

THE EFFECT ON FAMILY COMMUNICATION

The presence of technology in the home can also hinder effective communication between family members. Children, in particular, are susceptible to becoming overly dependent on their devices, which can lead to a lack of engagement with parents and siblings. This can create a divide in the family, as each member becomes absorbed in their own digital world.

Parents must be vigilant in monitoring their children's use of technology. It is crucial to set boundaries and establish rules for screen time to ensure that it does not interfere with family activities or relationships. By doing so, parents can help their children develop healthy habits and prevent technology from becoming a source of addiction or inappropriate content exposure.

FINDING BALANCE

To prevent technology from negatively impacting marriage and family life, couples need to establish clear guidelines for its use. This might include setting aside specific times during the day when devices are put away, such as during meals, family activities, or before bedtime. By creating these boundaries, couples can ensure that they remain connected and engaged with each other and their children.

Moreover, couples should make a conscious effort to engage in activities that foster intimacy and communication, such as taking walks together, having regular date nights, or participating in family outings without the distraction of phones or tablets.

In summary, while technology can enhance our lives in many ways, it is essential to be mindful of how it is used within the home. By setting boundaries and prioritizing personal interactions, couples and families can protect their relationships from the potential harm that excessive technology use can bring.

CHAPTER 5

FINANCIAL STEWARDSHIP IN MARRIAGE

BIBLICAL PRINCIPLES OF MONEY MANAGEMENT

Chapter Five
Financial Stewardship in Marriage
BIBLICAL PRINCIPLES OF MONEY MANAGEMENT

DEFINITION AND IMPORTANCE

Financial stewardship in marriage involves managing the financial resources that God has entrusted to a couple in a manner that honors Him. It includes earning, spending, saving, investing, and giving in a way that aligns with biblical principles. Proper financial stewardship is crucial for marital harmony and success. When managed well, finances can become a source of unity and growth rather than conflict and stress. The purpose of marriage is for the husband and wife to come together to become one in all things, therefore financial oneness is an essential element of the success of the victorious kingdom marriage.

FOUNDATIONS FOR MONEY MANAGEMENT

- **Ownership: Psalm 24:1 "The earth is the Lord's, and everything in it, the world, and all who live in it."** This verse emphasizes that everything belongs to God. Recognizing His ownership is the first step in financial stewardship. Couples should view themselves as managers, not owners, of their resources, and handle their finances with a sense of responsibility and accountability to God.

- **Work and Provision: Proverbs 13:11 "Dishonest money dwindles away, but whoever gathers money little by little makes it grow."** Hard work and honest labor are valued in the Bible. Couples are encouraged to earn their income through honest means and to be diligent in their efforts. Wealth accumulated gradually through honest work is more stable and sustainable.

- **Contentment: 1 Timothy 6:6-10 "But godliness with contentment is great gain. For we brought nothing into the world, and we can take nothing out of it. But if we have food and clothing, we will be content with that."** Contentment is key to financial stewardship. It helps couples avoid the pitfalls of materialism and greed. Recognizing that true wealth comes from a relationship with God and not from material possessions fosters a healthy attitude towards money.

- **Avoiding Debt: Proverbs 22:7 "The rich rule over the poor, and the borrower is slave to the lender."** This verse highlights the dangers of debt. While not all debt is avoidable, excessive or unnecessary debt can lead to financial bondage. Couples should strive to live within their means and avoid accumulating debt that could strain their finances and relationship.

- **Generosity: 2 Corinthians 9:6-7 "Remember this: Whoever sows sparingly will also reap sparingly, and whoever sows generously will also reap generously. Each of you should give what you have decided in your heart to give, not reluctantly or under compulsion, for God loves a cheerful giver." Generosity is a fundamental biblical principle. Giving is an act of worship and trust in God's provision. Couples are encouraged to give generously and cheerfully, supporting their church, charitable organizations, and those in need.

PRACTICAL STEPS FOR BIBLICAL MONEY MANAGEMENT

- **Recognize God's Ownership**

    Step: Begin by acknowledging that all financial resources belong to God. Pray together for wisdom and guidance in managing what He has entrusted to you.

    Application: Regularly remind yourselves that you are stewards of God's resources. This mindset will help you make financial decisions that honors Him.

- **Live Within Your Means**

    Step: Create a budget that aligns with your income and prioritize essential expenses such as housing, utilities, food, and transportation.

    Application: Avoid lifestyle inflation. Just because you can afford something doesn't mean you should buy it. Aim for simplicity and contentment in your spending habits.

- **Save and Invest Wisely**

    Step: Allocate a portion of your income to tithes and savings and investments. Build an emergency fund to cover unexpected expenses.

    Application: Research investment options and seek advice from financial professionals if needed. Plan for long-term goals such as retirement, children's education, and major purchases.

- **Give Generously**

    Step: Set aside a portion of your income for giving. Decide together which causes and organizations to support.

    Application: Regularly review and discuss your giving plan. Make generosity a central part of your financial stewardship, reflecting God's love and provision in your community.

- **Seek God's Guidance**

    Step: Regularly pray for wisdom in managing your finances. Invite God into your financial planning and decision-making processes.

    Application: Trust in God's provision and be open to His leading in how you use your resources. Faithfully steward your finances as an act of worship and obedience.

SCRIPTURAL EXAMPLES OF FINANCIAL STEWARDSHIP

- **Joseph in Egypt:** Genesis 41:33-36: "And now let Pharaoh look for a discerning and wise man and put him in charge of the land of Egypt. Let Pharaoh appoint commissioners over the land to take a fifth of the harvest of Egypt during the seven years of abundance. They should collect all the food of these good years that are coming and store up the grain under the authority of Pharaoh, to be kept in the cities for food. This food should be held in reserve for the country, to be used during the seven years of famine that will come upon Egypt, so that the country may not be ruined by the famine"

  Explanation: Joseph's prudent management during the years of abundance ensured Egypt's survival during the famine. His example teaches the importance of saving and planning for the future.

- **The Widow's Offering:** Mark 12:41-44: "Jesus sat down opposite the place where the offerings were put and watched the crowd putting their money into the temple treasury. Many rich people threw in large amounts. But a poor widow came and put in two very small copper coins, worth only a few cents. Calling his disciples to him, Jesus said, 'Truly I tell you, this poor widow has put more into the treasury than all the others. They all gave out of their wealth; but she, out of her poverty, put in everything—all she had to live on"

Explanation: The widow's offering exemplifies sacrificial giving and trust in God's provision. It's not the amount that matters but the heart and faith behind the giving.

Biblical principles of money management provide a solid foundation for financial stewardship in marriage. By recognizing God's ownership, living within their means, saving and investing wisely, giving generously, and seeking God's guidance, couples can manage their finances in a way that honors God and strengthens their relationship. Embracing these principles fosters unity in financial maturity, management, trust reflecting the love and provision of God in every aspect of married life.

Creating a Budget Together

Definition and Importance:

Creating a budget together is the process by which couples outline their income, expenses, savings, and financial goals. It serves as a financial roadmap that helps them manage their resources efficiently, avoid debt, and work towards common objectives. Budgeting is vital in marriage because it fosters transparency, mutual understanding, and accountability, ensuring both partners are on the same page financially.

STEPS TO CREATE A BUDGET TOGETHER

- **Gather Financial Information**

  Step: Collect all necessary financial documents, including pay stubs, bank statements, bills, and records of any other income or expenses.

  Application: This step involves full disclosure from both partners, ensuring that all sources of income and every expense are accounted for. Transparency is crucial to create an accurate and effective budget.

- **List All Expenses**

    Step: Categorize your expenses into fixed (rent/mortgage, utilities, loan payments) and variable (groceries, entertainment, dining out).

    Application: Break down expenses into specific categories to get a clear picture of where your money is going. This step helps identify areas where you can potentially cut costs or adjust spending.

- **Set Financial Goals**

    Step: Identify short-term (e.g., saving for a vacation) and long-term (e.g., buying a house, retirement) financial goals.

    Application: Discuss and agree on these goals as a couple. Setting clear and achievable goals provides motivation and a sense of direction for your budgeting efforts.

PRINCIPLES IN BUDGETING

- **Stewardship:** Luke 16:10-11: "Whoever can be trusted with very little can also be trusted with much, and whoever is dishonest with very little will also be dishonest with much. So if you have not been trustworthy in handling worldly wealth, who will trust you with true riches?"
    Explanation: Faithful stewardship involves managing resources wisely, regardless of the amount. Creating a budget reflects good stewardship by ensuring that financial resources are used effectively and responsibly.

- **Planning and Preparation:** Proverbs 21:5: "The plans of the diligent lead to profit as surely as haste leads to poverty."
    Explanation: Diligent planning, which includes budgeting, leads to financial stability and prosperity. Thoughtful preparation helps couples avoid financial pitfalls and make informed decisions.

- **Contentment:** Philippians 4:11-12: "I am not saying this because I am in need, for I have learned to be content whatever the circumstances. I know what it is to be in need, and I know what it is to have plenty. I have learned the secret of being content in any and every situation, whether well fed or hungry, whether living in plenty or in want."
- **Explanation:** Contentment plays a crucial role in budgeting. By being content with what they have, couples can avoid unnecessary spending and focus on their financial goals.

PRACTICAL TIPS FOR SUCCESSFUL BUDGETING

- **Communicate Openly**

    Tip: Regularly discuss your financial situation, goals, and any concerns.

    Application: Open communication ensures that both partners are involved in the budgeting process and helps prevent misunderstandings or conflicts about money.

- **Be Flexible**

    Tip: Allow for adjustments in your budget as circumstances change.

    Application: Life is unpredictable, and financial needs may shift. Being flexible with your budget allows you to adapt to new situations without stress.

- **Automate Savings**

    Tip: Set up automatic transfers to your savings accounts.

    Application: Automating savings helps you consistently save money without having to think about it, ensuring that you steadily work towards your financial goals.

- **Use Tools and Resources:**

    Tip: Take advantage of budgeting apps, financial planning software, and other resources.

    Application: These tools can simplify the budgeting process, provide insights into your spending habits, and help you stay on track.

- **Celebrate Milestones**

    Tip: Recognize and celebrate financial achievements, no matter how small.

    Application: Celebrating milestones, such as paying off a debt or reaching a savings goal, reinforces positive financial behavior and motivates you to continue making progress.

Creating a budget together is an essential practice for financial stewardship in marriage. It promotes transparency, accountability, and mutual understanding, helping couples manage their resources effectively. By following biblical principles and practical steps, couples can create a budget that aligns with their values, supports their goals, and strengthens their relationship. Through diligent planning, open communication, and a commitment to honoring God with their finances, couples can achieve financial stability and peace.

Generosity and Giving as a Couple
DEFINITION AND IMPORTANCE

Generosity in marriage involves the willingness to give time, resources, love, and support to each other, as well as to those in need outside the marriage. Giving as a couple refers to the joint efforts in sharing their blessings, whether through financial contributions, volunteer work, or acts of kindness. Embracing a lifestyle of generosity fosters a deeper connection between spouses, builds a legacy of compassion, and aligns with biblical teachings on stewardship and charity.

FOUNDATIONS FOR GENEROSITY

- **Principle of Sowing and Reaping:** 2 Corinthians 9:6-7: "Remember this: Whoever sows sparingly will also reap sparingly, and whoever sows generously will also reap generously. Each of you should give what you have decided in your heart to give, not reluctantly or under compulsion, for God loves a cheerful giver."
  Explanation: This passage emphasizes the principle that the measure of our generosity impacts the blessings we receive. It encourages giving from the heart, with joy and willingness, reflecting the true spirit of generosity.

- **Jesus' Teaching on Giving:** Luke 6:38: "Give, and it will be given to you. A good measure, pressed down, shaken together and running over, will be poured into your lap. For with the measure you use, it will be measured to you."
  Explanation: Jesus teaches that generosity brings abundant blessings. The act of giving creates a cycle of blessing that benefits both the giver and the recipient, encouraging couples to give freely and generously.

- **Example of Early Christians:** Acts 4:32-35: "All the believers were one in heart and mind. No one claimed that any of their possessions was their own, but they shared everything they had. With great power the apostles continued to testify to the resurrection of the Lord Jesus. And God's grace was so powerfully at work in them all that there were no needy persons among them. For from time to time those who owned land or houses sold them, brought the money from the sales and put it at the apostles' feet, and it was distributed to anyone who had need."
  Explanation: The early church exemplified communal generosity, where believers shared their possessions to ensure that no one was in need. This model of selflessness and community support is a powerful example for couples to follow in their giving.

TITHES AND OFFERINGS
THE FOUNDATION OF FINANCIAL STEWARDSHIP

Financial stewardship is not just about managing money wisely; it's about recognizing that all we have belongs to God and that we are merely stewards of His resources. One of the key aspects of this stewardship is the faithful practice of tithes and offerings to our home church where couples fellowship and receive spiritual food.

BIBLICAL BASIS FOR TITHING

Tithing, which means giving one-tenth of one's income, is a biblical principle that dates back to the Old Testament even before the laws of Moses during the days of father Abraham.

Gen 14:19 And he blessed him, and said, Blessed [be] Abram of the highest God, possessor of heaven and earth:
Gen 14:20 And blessed be the highest God, which hath delivered thine enemies into thy hand. And he gave him tithes of all.

Tithing is a principle which when neglected by married couples can hinder their financial unity and stability. Principles are laws which the Manufacturer places in his product to guarantee its success. The Lord wants to be the Lord over our finances so that He can destroy our dependence upon it. By walking in obedience of tithes, we are indeed surrendering our finances unto the Lord, and testifying that He is our Source.

Malachi 3:10, the Lord says, "Bring the whole tithe into the storehouse, that there may be food in my house. Test me in this," says the Lord Almighty, "and see if I will not throw open the floodgates of heaven and pour out so much blessing that there will not be room enough to store it." This passage not only underscores the importance of tithing but also comes with a promise of blessing for those who are faithful in its implementation. God does not need our money; He simply desires that we acknowledge with our obedience that He is the one who provides us with the means to acquire everything.

Mt 6:21 For where your treasure is, there will your heart be also.

Tithing is an act of obedience and trust in God. It acknowledges His lordship over our finances and demonstrates our reliance on His provision rather than our own understanding. By setting aside the first ten percent of our income for God's kingdom advancement in our home church, we put Him first in our financial lives, ensuring that our hearts are aligned with His will.

Pss 24:1 (KJV) The earth [is] the Lord's, and the fulness thereof; the world, and they that dwell therein.

OFFERINGS
While tithing is a fundamental principle, offerings are voluntary gifts given above and beyond the tithe. In **2 Corinthians 9:7, Paul writes, "Each of you should give what you have decided in your heart to give, not reluctantly or under compulsion, for God loves a cheerful giver."** Offerings are an expression of our love and gratitude to God. They allow us to participate in His work, whether through supporting our local church, helping the needy, or contributing to missions.

Offerings also serve as a reminder that our financial contributions are not just a duty but a privilege. They enable us to be part of something greater than ourselves, furthering the Kingdom of God on earth.

THE ROLE OF TITHES AND OFFERINGS IN MARRIAGE
For married couples, tithes and offerings should be a joint decision, reflecting their unity in financial matters and their shared commitment to God. This practice encourages couples to prioritize their spiritual lives together, building a foundation of trust and reliance on God's provision.

By faithfully giving tithes and offerings, couples can experience God's faithfulness in their finances. This spiritual discipline teaches them to live with open hands, trusting that God will meet their needs and provide for them abundantly. It also serves as a testimony to the world of God's goodness and faithfulness in their lives.

FINANCIAL STABILITY THROUGH FAITHFUL GIVING

One of the most profound ways to achieve financial stability is through faithful giving. When couples put God first in their finances, they invite His blessings into their lives. The practice of tithing and giving offerings keeps their hearts focused on God, guarding against greed and materialism. It also fosters a spirit of generosity, which can lead to greater financial freedom and peace.

Mal 3:10 Bring ye all the tithes into the storehouse, that there may be meat in mine house, and prove me now herewith, saith the Lord of hosts, if I will not open you the windows of heaven, and pour you out a blessing, that [there shall] not [be room] enough [to receive it].Mal 3:11 And I will rebuke the devourer for your sakes, and he shall not destroy the fruits of your ground; neither shall your vine cast her fruit before the time in the field, saith the Lord of hosts.

THE BLESSINGS OF TITHES AND OFFERINGS:

- The Lord promises to open the windows of heaven, meaning when couples withhold their tithes and offerings, they have basically decided to live their lives under a closed heaven.

- The Lord promises to rebuke the devourer for our sake, meaning God will make straight every crooked thing that has been consuming our finances.

- The Lord promises to not destroy the fruits of our ground, meaning, He alone will take pleasure in preserving the sources of your income, your jobs, businesses, and financial choices.

- The Lord promises that our vine will not cast her fruit before the time in the field, meaning the Lord will take our finances off life support, in other words couples will no longer live the stress of living from paycheck to paycheck.

Prov 3:9 Honor the Lord with thy substance, and with the first fruits of all thine increase: Prov 3:10 So shall thy barns be filled with plenty, and thy presses shall burst out with new wine.

In conclusion, tithes and offerings are not just financial transactions but acts of worship. They are an integral part of financial stewardship that allows couples to honor God with their resources and experience His blessings in their lives. By committing to this practice, couples can strengthen their faith, deepen their unity, and achieve true financial stability.

CHAPTER 6

Parenting And Family Life

Raising Children in a Godly Home

Chapter Six
Parenting And Family Life
Raising Children in a Godly Home

Raising children in a godly home involves nurturing them with Christian values and principles, ensuring their spiritual growth, and guiding them to develop a personal relationship with God. This process requires a holistic approach that encompasses spiritual, emotional, physical, and intellectual development, rooted in biblical teachings and a Christ-centered lifestyle.

FOUNDATIONS OF A GODLY HOME

- **Spiritual Leadership**: Parents are called to be spiritual leaders in their home, setting an example in faith and practice. The Bible emphasizes the importance of parents teaching their children about God's ways and His commandments. **Deuteronomy 6:6-7: "These commandments that I give you today are to be on your hearts. Impress them on your children. Talk about them when you sit at home and when you walk along the road, when you lie down and when you get up."**

- **Prayer and Worship**: Incorporating regular family prayers and worship times strengthens the spiritual bond and sets a routine of seeking God together. It demonstrates reliance on God and fosters a sense of community and belonging. **Philippians 4:6: "Do not be anxious about anything, but in every situation, by prayer and petition, with thanksgiving, present your requests to God."**

- **Biblical Education**: Teaching children the Word of God and helping them understand biblical truths is crucial. This includes reading Bible stories, memorizing scriptures, and discussing their applications in daily life. **2 Timothy 3:15: "And how from infancy you have known the Holy Scriptures, which are able to make you wise for salvation through faith in Christ Jesus."**

- **Modeling Christ-like Behavior**: Children learn by observing their parents. Demonstrating love, forgiveness, kindness, and humility in everyday interactions sets a powerful example for children to emulate. **Ephesians 4:32: "Be kind and compassionate to one another, forgiving each other, just as in Christ God forgave you."**

PRACTICAL STEPS FOR RAISING GODLY CHILDREN

- **Consistent Discipline with Love**: Discipline is an essential part of parenting, but it must be administered with love and care, aiming to correct and guide rather than punish. **Proverbs 13:24: "Whoever spares the rod hates their children, but the one who loves their children is careful to discipline them."**

- **Encouragement and Affirmation**: Positive reinforcement helps build a child's self-esteem and reinforces godly behavior. Regularly affirming your children's efforts and encouraging them fosters a nurturing environment. **1 Thessalonians 5:11: "Therefore encourage one another and build each other up, just as in fact you are doing."**

- **Involvement in Church Community**: Active participation in church activities, such as Sunday school, youth groups, and family services, provides children with a supportive faith community and additional spiritual mentors. **Hebrews 10:25: "Not giving up meeting together, as some are in the habit of doing, but encouraging one another—and all the more as you see the Day approaching."**

- **Teaching Service and Generosity**: Encouraging children to serve others and practice generosity instills a sense of empathy and compassion, aligning with the teachings of Jesus. **Acts 20:35: "In everything I did, I showed you that by this kind of hard work we must help the weak, remembering the words the Lord Jesus himself said: 'It is more blessed to give than to receive.'"**

- **Creating a Safe and Loving Environment**: A godly home should be a safe haven where children feel loved, accepted, and valued. This stability allows them to grow and explore their faith confidently. **Colossians 3:14: "And over all these virtues put on love, which binds them all together in perfect unity."**

CHALLENGES AND OVERCOMING THEM

- **Worldly Influences**: The external influences of society can often contradict biblical values. Parents need to be vigilant and proactive in discussing these influences with their children, guiding them to discern and choose wisely. **Romans 12:2: "Do not conform to the pattern of this world, but be transformed by the renewing of your mind. Then you will be able to test and approve what God's will is—his good, pleasing and perfect will."**

- **Balancing Work and Family Time**: In today's busy world, balancing work responsibilities with family time can be challenging. Prioritizing family devotion and quality time together is essential. **Ephesians 5:16: "Making the most of every opportunity, because the days are evil."**

- **Dealing with Rebellion**: There may be times when children rebel against the teachings and values of a godly home. Patience, persistent prayer, and open communication are key in navigating these periods. **Galatians 6:9: "Let us not become weary in doing good, for at the proper time we will reap a harvest if we do not give up."**

Raising children in a godly home is a dynamic and ongoing process that requires dedication, intentionality, and reliance on God. By laying a strong spiritual foundation, parents can guide their children to grow into faithful and godly individuals who will carry forward the legacy of faith into future generations. The journey is challenging, but the rewards are eternal, as children raised in godly homes have the potential to make a profound impact on the world for Christ.

Balancing Marriage and Parenting

Balancing marriage and parenting involve managing the dual roles of being a loving spouse and a dedicated parent. It requires finding harmony between nurturing your marital relationship and fulfilling your responsibilities as parents. This balance is essential for a healthy, thriving family dynamic where both the marriage and the parent-child relationships are given the attention and care they need.

IMPORTANCE OF BALANCING MARRIAGE AND PARENTING

- **Strengthening the Marital Bond**: A strong marriage creates a stable foundation for the entire family. When parents prioritize their relationship, they model love, respect, and cooperation for their children. **Ephesians 5:25: "Husbands, love your wives, just as Christ loved the church and gave himself up for her."**

- **Creating a Secure Environment for Children**: Children feel more secure and thrive better in an environment where their parents have a healthy and loving relationship. **Proverbs 22:6: "Start children off on the way they should go, and even when they are old, they will not turn from it."**

- **Preventing Parental Burnout**: Balancing these roles helps prevent burnout, ensuring that both parents can maintain their physical, emotional, and spiritual health. **Matthew 11:28: "Come to me, all you who are weary and burdened, and I will give you rest."**

PRACTICAL STRATEGIES FOR BALANCING MARRIAGE AND PARENTING

- **Prioritize Your Marriage**: Make your marriage a priority by setting aside regular time for each other. Date nights, weekend getaways, or even a few quiet moments together each day can reinforce your bond. **Song of Solomon 2:10: "My beloved spoke and said to me, 'Arise, my darling, my beautiful one, come with me"**

- **Effective Communication**: Maintain open and honest communication with your spouse about your needs, challenges, and expectations. Regularly discuss how to support each other in your parenting roles and marital relationship. **Ephesians 4:15: "Instead, speaking the truth in love, we will grow to become in every respect the mature body of him who is the head, that is, Christ."**

- **Shared Responsibilities**: Share parenting and household responsibilities to ensure that neither partner feels overwhelmed. This teamwork approach can enhance mutual respect and cooperation. **Ecclesiastes 4:9: "Two are better than one, because they have a good return for their labor."**

- **Intentional Family Time**: While it's crucial to spend time as a couple, it's also important to have regular family activities that everyone enjoys. This reinforces family bonds and creates lasting memories. **Joshua 24:15: "But as for me and my household, we will serve the Lord."**

- **Seek Support and Community**: Don't hesitate to seek support from extended family, friends, or church communities. Engaging in a supportive community can provide additional resources and encouragement. **Galatians 6:2: "Carry each other's burdens, and in this way, you will fulfill the law of Christ."**

- **Self-Care**: Prioritize self-care for both parents. Physical, emotional, and spiritual well-being is crucial to effectively manage both marriage and parenting responsibilities. **1 Corinthians 6:19-20: "Do you not know that your bodies are temples of the Holy Spirit, who is in you, whom you have received from God? You are not your own; you were bought at a price. Therefore, honor God with your bodies."**

- **Spiritual Growth Together**: Engage in spiritual activities together, such as praying, attending church, and studying the Bible. This not only strengthens your marriage but also sets a spiritual example for your children. **Matthew 18:20: "For where two or three gather in my name, there am I with them."**

OVERCOMING CHALLENGES

- **Time Constraints**: Busy schedules can make it challenging to balance marriage and parenting. Prioritizing and scheduling specific times for your spouse and children can help manage this. **Psalm 90:12: "Teach us to number our days, that we may gain a heart of wisdom."**

- **Parenting Differences**: Couples may have different parenting styles or approaches. Open communication and mutual respect are key to finding a balanced approach that works for both parents. **Amos 3:3: "Do two walks together unless they have agreed to do so?"**

- **Stress and Fatigue**: Parenting can be exhausting, leading to stress and fatigue. Ensuring that both parents get adequate rest and support can alleviate these challenges. **Isaiah 40:31: "But those who hope in the Lord will renew their strength. They will soar on wings like eagles; they will run and not grow weary; they will walk and not faint."**

BENEFITS OF BALANCING MARRIAGE AND PARENTING

- **Stronger Family Unity**: A well-balanced approach fosters a cohesive and harmonious family unit where love and respect are prevalent. **Psalm 133:1: "How good and pleasant it is when God's people live together in unity!"**

- **Healthy Child Development**: Children raised in an environment where their parents maintain a strong relationship tend to develop better emotionally and socially. **Proverbs 1:8-9: "Listen, my son, to your father's instruction and do not forsake your mother's teaching. They are a garland to grace your head and a chain to adorn your neck."**

- **Enhanced Marital Satisfaction**: Couples who balance their roles well often experience higher levels of marital satisfaction and intimacy. **1 Peter 3:7: "Husbands, in the same way, be considerate as you live with your wives, and treat them with respect as the weaker partner and as heirs with you of the gracious gift of life, so that nothing will hinder your prayers."**

Balancing marriage and parenting is a continuous and intentional effort that requires dedication, communication, and mutual support. By prioritizing both roles and relying on biblical principles, couples can create a nurturing and harmonious family environment. This balance not only strengthens the marital relationship but also provides children with a stable and loving foundation, guiding them to grow into well-rounded individuals who reflect the values and teachings of their faith.

Uniformity in Parenting a Blended Family
HOW TO PARENT A BLENDED FAMILY IN MARRIAGE?

Parenting in a blended family comes with unique challenges and opportunities. When a man and a woman enter a marriage with children from previous relationships, they must work together to create a unified, loving environment where all children feel valued and accepted. This process requires intentional effort, mutual respect, and a commitment to shared parenting responsibilities.

In a blended family, it is essential to approach parenting with the understanding that all children, regardless of their biological connections, are equally important. Recognizing and addressing the unique needs of each child while fostering a sense of unity and belonging within the family is crucial. Both parents must be aligned in their approach to discipline, rules, and family values to prevent confusion and conflict.

When my wife and I got married, we each brought four children into the marriage. My children became her children, and her children became mine. I met her with a 14-year-old boy and a 3-month-old baby, whom I have now adopted and given my last name. This is how it's supposed to be, but many couples struggle with uniting in parenting their blended family, leading to serious problems within their marriages.

One of the critical aspects of successful blended family parenting is mutual acceptance and respect. This means that each parent must embrace the role of co-parent to all the children in the household, regardless of their biological relationship. For instance, a husband should be able to correct his wife's children from a previous relationship, and the wife should be able to discipline the husband's children. This uniformity ensures that all children receive consistent guidance and support.

The Bible provides valuable insights into family dynamics and the importance of unity and love within the household. **Ephesians 6:4** advises, **"Fathers, do not exasperate your children; instead, bring them up in the training and instruction of the Lord."** This scripture emphasizes the importance of nurturing and guiding children with love and consistency.

Additionally, **Colossians 3:21** states, **"Fathers, do not embitter your children, or they will become discouraged."** This verse highlights the need for fair and loving discipline, which is essential in a blended family where children may be adjusting to new family structures and dynamics.

PRACTICAL TIPS FOR PARENTING A BLENDED FAMILY

- **Open Communication:** Discuss parenting styles and expectations openly before blending families. Make sure both parties understand and agree on how to handle various parenting scenarios.

- **Unified Discipline:** Present a united front when it comes to discipline. Children need to see that both parents support and enforce the same rules. This consistency helps children feel secure and understand what is expected of them. Inconsistency in this area will open a door where the children could use manipulation tactics in order to achieve their own selflessness. Children are the first to recognize their parents' division, especially in the area of discipline.

- **Respect and Acceptance:** Teach children to respect and accept all family members. Encourage bonding activities that help build relationships among step-siblings.

- **Consistency is Key:** Consistency in rules and discipline helps children feel secure and understand what is expected of them. Establish clear household rules and ensure both parents adhere to them.

- **Parental Support:** Support each other in your parenting roles. Do not undermine or contradict your spouse in front of the children. Show a united front, and back each other up in decisions.

- **Seek External Support:** Sometimes, seeking advice from a family counselor or attending blended family support groups can provide valuable insights and strategies. Professional guidance can help navigate complex family dynamics and foster unity.

- **Spend Quality Time Together:** Make time for family activities that include everyone. This helps to build a sense of belonging and togetherness. Plan regular family outings, game nights, or meals where everyone participates.

- **Individual Attention:** Recognize and address the unique needs of each child. Spend one-on-one time with each child to understand their feelings and build a strong relationship.

- **Foster Mutual Respect:** Encourage children to respect their step-siblings and step-parents. Model respectful behavior yourself. Teach them that respect is a foundational value in your family.

- **Prayer and Spiritual Guidance:** Integrate prayer and spiritual activities into your family routine. Praying together can strengthen family bonds and provide a sense of peace and guidance.

In our experience, one of the key lessons is the importance of seeing each other's children as your own. This mindset helps in building a cohesive family unit. When children see that both parents are committed to their well-being, it fosters trust and respect.

Another important lesson is the need for patience and understanding. Blending families takes time, and there will be challenges along the way. It's essential to be patient with each other and with the children as everyone adjusts to the new family structure.

Blended family parenting requires patience, understanding, and a willingness to adapt. By approaching it with love and a commitment to unity, couples can create a stable, nurturing environment where all children thrive. This journey, while challenging, can ultimately strengthen the family bond and create a lasting legacy of love and togetherness.

Through open communication, unified discipline, and mutual respect, blended families can overcome the challenges they face and build a strong, loving family unit. The journey may be difficult, but with God's guidance and a commitment to each other, it is possible to create a harmonious and fulfilling family life.

BUILDING A LEGACY OF FAITH

Building a legacy of faith means creating a lasting spiritual heritage within your family that endures through generations. This involves instilling strong Christian values, beliefs, and practices in your children and future descendants. It is about nurturing a deep, abiding faith in God that influences their lives and decisions, ensuring that your faith continues to shape and guide your family long after you are gone.

IMPORTANCE OF BUILDING A LEGACY OF FAITH

- **Spiritual Continuity**: Ensures that the faith and values you hold dear are passed down to future generations, creating a lineage of believers. **Deuteronomy 6:6-7: "These commandments that I give you today are to be on your hearts. Impress them on your children. Talk about them when you sit at home and when you walk along the road, when you lie down and when you get up."**

- **Moral Foundation**: Provides a strong moral foundation for children, helping them navigate life's challenges with biblical principles. **Proverbs 22:6: "Start children off on the way they should go, and even when they are old, they will not turn from it."**

- **Community and Belonging**: Fosters a sense of belonging and identity within a community of faith, helping children feel connected to a larger family of believers. **Psalm 145:4: "One generation commends your works to another; they tell of your mighty acts."**

- **Resilience and Hope**: Instills resilience and hope in children, teaching them to rely on God during difficult times. **Romans 15:13: "May the God of hope fill you with all joy and peace as you trust in him, so that you may overflow with hope by the power of the Holy Spirit."**

PRACTICAL STEPS TO BUILDING A LEGACY OF FAITH

- **Live Out Your Faith**: Model a genuine, active faith in your daily life. Children learn by observing, so demonstrate love, patience, forgiveness, and devotion to God. **1 Corinthians 11:1: "Follow my example, as I follow the example of Christ."**

- **Teach Biblical Principles**: Regularly teach your children about God's Word. Use everyday moments to discuss biblical truths and apply them to real-life situations. **Deuteronomy 11:19: "Teach them to your children, talking about them when you sit at home and when you walk along the road, when you lie down and when you get up."**

- **Pray Together**: Make prayer a central part of your family life. Pray together regularly, teaching your children to depend on God in all circumstances. **Philippians 4:6: "Do not be anxious about anything, but in every situation, by prayer and petition, with thanksgiving, present your requests to God."**

- **Attend Church Together**: Regularly attend church as a family to worship, learn, and grow in faith together. This also helps build a strong community support system. **Hebrews 10:25: "Not giving up meeting together, as some are in the habit of doing, but encouraging one another—and all the more as you see the Day approaching."**

- **Serve Together**: Engage in acts of service as a family, demonstrating the importance of loving and helping others. This reinforces the biblical principle of serving one another in love. **Galatians 5:13: "You, my brothers and sisters, were called to be free. But do not use your freedom to indulge the flesh; rather, serve one another humbly in love."**

- **Create Faith Traditions**: Establish family traditions that reinforce faith, such as daily devotions, celebrating religious holidays with spiritual focus, and discussing what everyone is thankful for during meals. **Joshua 24:15: "But as for me and my household, we will serve the Lord."**

- **Encourage Personal Faith**: Encourage each child to develop their own personal relationship with God, fostering a sense of ownership of their faith. **2 Timothy 1:5: "I am reminded of your sincere faith, which first lived in your grandmother Lois and in your mother Eunice and, I am persuaded, now lives in you also."**

OVERCOMING CHALLENGES

- **Cultural Influences**: In a society with diverse beliefs and values, it can be challenging to maintain a strong Christian identity. Reinforce the importance of biblical values despite societal pressures. **Romans 12:2: "Do not conform to the pattern of this world, but be transformed by the renewing of your mind. Then you will be able to test and approve what God's will is—his good, pleasing and perfect will."**

- **Busy Schedules**: The demands of modern life can make it difficult to prioritize faith activities. Intentionally set aside time for family worship, Bible study, and prayer. **Matthew 6:33: "But seek first his kingdom and his righteousness, and all these things will be given to you as well."**

- **Interpersonal Conflicts**: Family disagreements can disrupt spiritual activities. Emphasize the importance of forgiveness and reconciliation as central to your faith. **Ephesians 4:32: "Be kind and compassionate to one another, forgiving each other, just as in Christ God forgave you."**

BENEFITS OF BUILDING A LEGACY OF FAITH

- **Long-term Spiritual Health**: Ensures that future generations have a strong foundation in Christ, enabling them to live lives that honor God. **Psalm 78:4: "We will not hide them from their descendants; we will tell the next generation the praiseworthy deeds of the Lord, his power, and the wonders he has done."**

- **Unified Family Vision**: Creates a shared vision and purpose for the family, fostering unity and a common goal of glorifying God. **Proverbs 29:18: "Where there is no vision, the people perish: but he that keepeth the law, happy is he."**

- **Increased Family Resilience**: Builds resilience as the family learns to rely on God and each other during challenging times, reinforcing the importance of faith. **Isaiah 40:31: "But those who hope in the Lord will renew their strength. They will soar on wings like eagles; they will run and not grow weary; they will walk and not faint."**

Building a legacy of faith is a deliberate and ongoing effort that requires dedication, intentionality, and reliance on God's guidance. By living out your faith, teaching biblical principles, praying together, and creating faith-centered traditions, you can establish a strong spiritual heritage that impacts your family for generations. This legacy not only benefits your immediate family but also contributes to the broader community of believers, ensuring that the light of Christ continues to shine brightly in the world.

CHAPTER 7

Facing Trials And Growing Together

Trusting God in Difficult Times

Chapter Seven
Facing Trials and Growing Together
Trusting God in Difficult Times

THE REALITY OF TRIALS IN MARRIAGE

Marriage is the vehicle through which God intends to showcase His glory on earth through the human family. As such, there is a strategic target on the backs of all marriages and family structures. Trials and difficulties are inevitable parts of life, and marriage is no exception. These challenges can range from financial struggles, health issues, and loss of loved ones, to more personal conflicts like misunderstandings and emotional disconnects. However, it is during these tough times that trusting God becomes crucial for the survival and growth of a marriage.

UNDERSTANDING THE PURPOSE OF TRIALS
God uses trials to refine and strengthen us. **James 1:2-4 says, "Consider it pure joy, my brothers and sisters, whenever you face trials of many kinds, because you know that the testing of your faith produces perseverance. Let perseverance finish its work so that you may be mature and complete, not lacking anything."** In the context of marriage, trials can deepen our faith, enhance our character, and fortify our bond with our spouse.

TRUSTING GOD'S SOVEREIGNTY
Trusting God in difficult times begins with recognizing His sovereignty. God is in control of all circumstances, and nothing happens without His knowledge or permission. Married couples should always remember that marriage is the Lord's product for the purpose of using the human family to influence the earth. Romans 8:28 assures us, "And we know that in all things God works for the good of those who love him, who have been called according to his purpose." Even when situations seem bleak, we can trust that God is working behind the scenes for our good and His glory.

PRACTICAL STEPS TO TRUSTING GOD

- **Prayer:** Prayer is a powerful tool in building trust in God. **Philippians 4:6-7 encourages us, "Do not be anxious about anything, but in every situation, by prayer and petition, with thanksgiving, present your requests to God. And the peace of God, which transcends all understanding, will guard your hearts and your minds in Christ Jesus."** Couples should make it a habit to pray together, seeking God's guidance and strength during trials.

- **Studying Scripture:** The Bible is a manual for the marriage product which secures comfort and guidance. **Psalms 119:105 says, "Your word is a lamp for my feet, a light on my path."** Regularly reading and meditating on God's word helps to remind us of His promises and faithfulness.

- **Encouraging One Another:** In times of difficulty, spouses should support and encourage each other. **Hebrews 10:24-25 states, "And let us consider how we may spur** one another on toward love and good deeds, not giving up meeting together, as some are in the habit of doing, but encouraging one another—and all the more as you see the Day approaching." Encouragement can come through kind words, acts of service, or simply being present for each other.

- **Maintaining a Perspective of Faith:** It's essential to maintain a perspective of faith rather than fear. **2 Corinthians 5:7 tells us, "For we live by faith, not by sight."** Trusting God means believing that He will see us through the storm and that there is a purpose behind every trial. **1Pet 1:7 That the trial of your faith, being much more precious than of gold that perisheth, though it be tried with fire, might be found unto praise and honor and glory at the appearing of Jesus Christ:**

EXAMPLES OF TRUST IN THE BIBLE

The Bible is filled with examples of individuals who trusted God during difficult times. Abraham trusted God when asked to sacrifice his son Isaac (Genesis 22). Job maintained his faith despite losing everything (Job 1-2). Ruth showed loyalty and faith in God by sticking with Naomi and eventually becoming part of the lineage of Christ (Ruth 1-4). These stories serve as reminders that God is faithful and trustworthy, even in the most challenging circumstances.

Trusting God in difficult times is not always easy, but it is essential for a strong and resilient marriage. By praying together, studying Scriptures, encouraging one another, and maintaining a perspective of faith, couples can navigate the storms of life with confidence in God's sovereign plan. Remembering that God uses trials to refine and strengthen us can provide hope and purpose during tough times, ultimately bringing glory to God through the union of marriage.

Strengthening Your Marriage Through Adversity
THE INEVITABILITY OF ADVERSITY

Adversity is an unavoidable part of life and marriage. Challenges such as financial difficulties, health crises, job loss, and personal conflicts can test the strength of a marital relationship. However, these adversities also offer opportunities for growth and deeper connection between spouses. A marriage that endures and strengthens through adversity is one that is built on a solid foundation. **Mt 7:24 Therefore whosoever heareth these sayings of mine, and doeth them, I will liken him unto a wise man, which built his house upon a rock:**

Mt 7:25 And the rain descended, and the floods came, and the winds blew, and beat upon that house; and it fell not: for it was founded upon a rock.

EMBRACING A GROWTH MINDSET

One of the keys to strengthening your marriage through adversity is to adopt a growth mindset. This means viewing challenges as opportunities for personal and relational development rather than insurmountable obstacles. **James 1:2-4 encourages us to "consider it pure joy, my brothers and sisters, whenever you face trials of many kinds, because you know that the testing of your faith produces perseverance."** By embracing adversity as a chance to grow, couples can build resilience and a stronger bond.

COMMUNICATION AND TRANSPARENCY

Open and honest communication is vital during times of adversity. Couples must share their feelings, fears, and concerns with each other to foster understanding and support. **Ephesians 4:15 advises us to "speak the truth in love,"** which is crucial during tough times. This involves not only expressing oneself but also listening empathetically to one's spouse. Transparency helps to build trust and ensures that both partners are on the same page, working together to overcome challenges.

LEANING ON EACH OTHER'S STRENGTHS

Every individual has unique strengths and weaknesses. In a marriage, it is important to recognize and lean on each other's strengths during adversity. **Ecclesiastes 4:9-10 states, "Two are better than one, because they have a good return for their labor: If either of them falls down, one can help the other up."** By complementing each other's strengths, couples can tackle problems more effectively and support one another through difficult times.

MAINTAINING UNITY

Prov 24:10 [If] thou faint in the day of adversity, thy strength [is] small.

Adversity can sometimes drive a wedge between spouses, leading to blame and conflict. It is crucial to maintain unity and remember that you are a team. **Mark 10:8 reminds us that "the two will become one flesh. So, they are no longer two, but one flesh."** Facing challenges together with a united front can strengthen the marital bond and ensure that both partners feel supported and valued.

DEVELOPING A SUPPORT SYSTEM

Having a strong support system outside of marriage is also beneficial. Trusted friends, family members, or a faith community can provide additional support, encouragement, and perspective. **Proverbs 11:14 notes that "where there is no guidance, a people fall, but in an abundance of counselors there is safety."** A support system can offer practical help, emotional support, and spiritual guidance during tough times.

PRACTICING PATIENCE AND FORGIVENESS

Adversity often brings out the best and worst in people. Practicing patience and forgiveness is essential for navigating these times without lasting damage to the relationship. **Colossians 3:13 urges us to "bear with each other and forgive one another if any of you has a grievance against someone. Forgive as the Lord forgave you."** Holding on to grudges or being impatient can exacerbate problems, whereas forgiveness and patience can foster healing and growth.

KEEPING THE FAITH

Faith plays a crucial role in navigating adversity. Trusting in God's plan and leaning on His strength can provide comfort and direction. **Isaiah 41:10 reassures us, "So do not fear, for I am with you; do not be dismayed, for I am your God. I will strengthen you and help you; I will uphold you with my righteous right hand."** Prayer, worship, and consistent bible studies focused on rising issues can help couples stay connected to God and each other during difficult times.

INVESTING IN THE RELATIONSHIP

During adversity, it is easy to become consumed by the problem at hand and neglect the relationship. It is important to continue investing in the marriage by spending quality time together, showing affection, and maintaining intimacy. Ephesians 5:25-28 encourages husbands to love their wives as Christ loved the church and gave Himself up for her, highlighting the importance of sacrificial love and care in a marriage.

SEEKING PROFESSIONAL HELP

Sometimes, the challenges faced in marriage require professional help. Seeking counseling or therapy can provide couples with the tools and strategies needed to navigate adversity effectively. **Proverbs 19:20 advises, "Listen to advice and accept instruction, that you may gain wisdom in the future."** Professional guidance can help couples address deep-seated issues and develop healthier communication and coping mechanisms.

CELEBRATING SMALL VICTORIES

In the midst of adversity, it is important to celebrate small victories. Recognizing and appreciating the progress made, no matter how small, can boost morale and reinforce the bond between spouses. Philippians 4:8 encourages us to focus on whatever is true, noble, right, pure, lovely, admirable, excellent, or praiseworthy. Celebrating small victories helps to maintain a positive outlook and reinforces the strength of the relationship.

Strengthening your marriage through adversity requires a combination of faith, communication, unity, patience, and ongoing investment in the relationship. By adopting a growth mindset, leaning on each other's strengths, maintaining a support system, and seeking professional help, when necessary, couples can navigate challenges together and emerge stronger. Trusting in God and celebrating small victories along the way further reinforce the marital bond, ensuring that the marriage not only survives but thrives through adversity.

Encouraging Each Other's Spiritual Gifts
UNDERSTANDING SPIRITUAL GIFTS

Spiritual gifts are unique abilities given by the Holy Spirit to believers for the purpose of building up the church and glorifying God. These gifts vary from teaching and prophecy to healing and hospitality. Recognizing and nurturing these gifts within a marriage is crucial for both personal and spiritual growth. **1 Corinthians 12:4-6 states, "There are different kinds of gifts, but the same Spirit distributes them. There are different kinds of service, but the same Lord. There are different kinds of working, but in all of them and in everyone it is the same God at work."**

IDENTIFYING EACH OTHER'S GIFTS

The first step in encouraging each other's spiritual gifts is identifying them. This can be done through prayer, conversation, and observation. **Ephesians 4:11-12 explains that God has given different gifts to different people: "So Christ himself gave the apostles, the prophets, the evangelists, the pastors and teachers, to equip his people for works of service,** so that the body of Christ may be built up." Understanding and acknowledging each other's gifts is essential for mutual support and growth.

AFFIRMING AND VALUING GIFTS
Once identified, it is important to affirm and value each other's gifts. This involves expressing appreciation and encouragement, recognizing the significance of each gift, and showing gratitude for how these gifts contribute to the marriage and the broader community. **Romans 12:10 encourages believers to "Be devoted to one another in love. Honor one another above yourselves."** Valuing each other's gifts fosters a supportive and loving environment where both partners can thrive.

PROVIDING OPPORTUNITIES FOR GROWTH
Encouraging each other's spiritual gifts involves providing opportunities for growth and development. This can include participating in church activities, joining small groups or Bible studies, and engaging in community service. **Hebrews 10:24-25 urges believers to "consider how we may spur one another on toward love and good deeds, not giving up meeting together, as some are in the habit of doing, but encouraging one another—and all the more as you see the Day approaching."** Creating an environment where both partners can use and develop their gifts is crucial for spiritual growth.

SUPPORTING EACH OTHER IN MINISTRY
Supporting each other in ministry means being actively involved in each other's spiritual journey. This can involve helping with preparations, attending events, and offering emotional and practical support. **Galatians 6:2 instructs us to "Carry each other's burdens, and in this way, you will fulfill the law of Christ."** By supporting each other's ministry efforts, couples can strengthen their bond and work together to serve God and their community.

ENCOURAGING CONTINUOUS LEARNING
Encouraging continuous learning and spiritual growth is another key aspect of fostering each other's spiritual gifts. This can be done through reading and studying the Bible together, attending seminars and workshops, and seeking mentorship from more experienced believers. **2 Timothy 2:15 advises, "Do your best to present yourself to God as one approved, a worker who does not need to be ashamed and who correctly handles the word of truth."** Continuous learning helps couples to deepen their understanding of their gifts and how to use them effectively.

PRAYING FOR EACH OTHER'S GIFTS
Prayer is a powerful tool for encouraging each other's spiritual gifts. Praying for each other's growth, wisdom, and strength can help couples stay connected to God and each other. **James 5:16 emphasizes the importance of prayer: "Therefore confess your sins to each other and pray for each other so that you may be healed. The prayer of a righteous person is powerful and effective."** Regularly praying for each other's gifts can lead to greater spiritual unity and effectiveness.

CELEBRATING EACH OTHER'S SUCCESSES
Celebrating each other's successes in using their spiritual gifts is vital for encouragement and motivation. Acknowledging and rejoicing in each other's

achievements, no matter how small, can foster a positive and supportive atmosphere. **1 Thessalonians 5:11 urges believers to "encourage one another and build each other up, just as in fact you are doing."** Celebrating successes helps to reinforce the value of each other's contributions and motivates continued growth and service.

CULTIVATING HUMILITY AND PATIENCE

Cultivating humility and patience is essential when encouraging each other's spiritual gifts. Understanding that growth and development take time and being patient with each other's progress is crucial. **Philippians 2:3-4 advises, "Do nothing out of selfish ambition or vain conceit. Rather, in humility value others above yourselves, not looking to your own interests but each of you to the interests of the others."** Practicing humility and patience helps to create a nurturing and supportive environment.

SEEKING GOD'S GUIDANCE TOGETHER

Seeking God's guidance together in how to best use and develop each other's spiritual gifts is crucial. This involves praying together, seeking wisdom from the Bible, and listening for the Holy Spirit's direction. **Proverbs 3:5-6 encourages believers to "Trust in the Lord with all your heart and lean not on your own understanding; in all your ways submit to him, and he will make your paths straight."** By seeking God's guidance, couples can ensure that they are using their gifts according to His will and purpose.

CREATING A LEGACY OF SERVICE

Encouraging each other's spiritual gifts contributes to creating a legacy of service and faithfulness. As couples work together to develop and use their gifts, they set an example for their children, friends, and community. **1 Peter 4:10-11 reminds believers, "Each of you should use whatever gift you have received to serve others, as faithful stewards of God's grace in its various forms. If anyone speaks, they should do so as one who speaks the very words of God. If anyone serves, they should do so with the strength God provides, so that in all things God may be praised through Jesus Christ."** Building a legacy of service not only strengthens the marriage but also impacts future generations.

Encouraging each other's spiritual gifts is a vital aspect of a strong and God-centered marriage. By identifying, valuing, and nurturing each other's gifts, couples can grow together spiritually and strengthen their relationship. Providing opportunities for growth, supporting each other in ministry, encouraging continuous learning, praying for each other's gifts, celebrating successes, and seeking God's guidance together are all crucial components of this process. Cultivating humility, patience, and a legacy of service further reinforce the marital bond and ensure that the marriage reflects God's love and purpose.

CHAPTER 8

SERVING GOD AND RENEWING COMMITMENT

FINDING YOUR JOINT MINISTRY

Chapter Eight
Serving God and Renewing Commitment
Finding Your Joint Ministry

UNDERSTANDING MARRIAGE AS GOD'S PRODUCT

One of the common mistakes many married couples make is approaching marriage as their personal endeavor or product. However, marriage should be seen as the product of God—a covenant made between two people before God, intended to be used for His earthly expression. This divine perspective transforms how couples view their union, guiding them to understand that marriage is not just about personal happiness but about fulfilling God's purpose.

Hebrews 13:4 reminds us, **"Marriage is honorable among all, and the bed undefiled; but fornicators and adulterers God will judge."** This scripture emphasizes the sanctity of marriage as an institution created by God, worthy of respect and honor. The focus here is not solely on the husband and wife but on the institution itself, which belongs to the King and His kingdom.

When the enemy attacks marriages, his target is not merely the individuals but the vows made before God. The devil aims to cause husbands and wives to break their covenant, thereby disrupting God's plan for their union. Recognizing that God is the third party in every marriage is crucial because only He can preserve it from all forms of attacks.

Ecclesiastes 4:12 states, **"Though one may be overpowered, two can defend themselves. A cord of three strands is not quickly broken."** This verse underscores the strength of a marriage rooted in God. With God as the third strand, the bond between husband and wife becomes unbreakable.

COMMON MISTAKES IN MARRIAGE

Many couples invest significant effort in ensuring a perfect wedding celebration but neglect their spiritual lives afterward. They often stop attending church together, missing out on the spiritual foundation that strengthens their marriage. This disconnect can lead to a gradual weakening of their bond, making them more susceptible to the enemy's attacks.

IMPORTANCE OF CHURCH AND MINISTRY

Active participation in church and ministry plays a crucial role in sustaining a strong and healthy marriage. Being involved in church activities together helps couples grow spiritually and strengthens their bond. It provides a platform to serve God together, reinforcing their shared purpose and commitment.

- **Strengthening the Spiritual Foundation**
  The church plays a pivotal role in nurturing the spiritual growth of individuals and couples. For a marriage to thrive, it is essential that both partners have a strong spiritual foundation. Regular church attendance and participation in ministry activities provide couples with the spiritual nourishment and guidance necessary to deepen their relationship with God and each other. **Hebrews 10:25** states. **"Not forsaking the assembling of ourselves together, as the manner of some is; but exhorting one another: and so much the more, as ye see the day approaching."** This verse highlights the importance of gathering together with other believers for mutual encouragement and spiritual growth. When couples engage in church activities together, they are more likely to grow spiritually and strengthen their marriage bond.

- **Building a Supportive Community**
  The church community offers a network of support for married couples. It provides a safe space where couples can share their experiences, seek advice, and receive encouragement from others who are on similar journeys. This sense of community is vital for maintaining a healthy and resilient marriage. Proverbs 27:17 says. **"Iron sharpens iron, and one man sharpens another."** This proverb underscores the importance of community and mutual support. In the context of marriage, being part of a church community helps couples stay accountable, receive wise counsel, and be encouraged in their walk with God.

- **Opportunities for Joint Ministry**
  Engaging in ministry together allows couples to serve God and others, fostering a sense of purpose and unity. Ministry activities can include volunteering in church programs, participating in outreach missions, or leading small groups. These shared experiences not only strengthen the couple's bond but also provide opportunities for personal and spiritual growth. **Ephesians 2:10** states. **"For we are his workmanship, created in Christ Jesus unto good works, which God hath before ordained that we should walk in them."** This verse reminds us that God has prepared good works for us to do, and for married couples, serving together in ministry is a powerful way to fulfill this calling.

- **Enhancing Communication and Understanding**
  Serving in church and ministry requires effective communication and teamwork. Couples who engage in these activities together learn to communicate better, understand each other's strengths and weaknesses, and work collaboratively towards common goals. These skills are invaluable in building a strong and healthy marriage.

- **Modeling a Christ-Centered Life**
  When couples are actively involved in church and ministry, they model a Christ-centered life for their children, family, and community. This witness can have a profound impact on others, demonstrating the importance of faith and commitment in marriage. **Matthew 5:16** says. **"Let your light shine before men, that they may see your good works, and glorify your Father which is in heaven."** By participating in church and ministry, couples let their light shine, bringing glory to God and inspiring others to follow their example.

- **Protecting Against Spiritual Attacks**
  Active involvement in church and ministry helps couples stay spiritually vigilant and resilient against the enemy's attacks. The enemy often targets marriages, knowing that a strong, godly marriage is a powerful testimony to God's love and faithfulness. By staying connected to the church and serving together, couples can fortify their marriage against these spiritual attacks. **1 Peter 5:8 warns, "Be sober, be vigilant; because your adversary the devil, as a roaring lion, walketh about, seeking whom he may devour."** Regular participation in church activities and ministry keeps couples spiritually alert and prepared to resist the enemy's schemes. The importance of church and ministry in marriage cannot be overstated. Regular church attendance, active participation in ministry, and engagement in a supportive church community provide couples with the spiritual foundation, support, and opportunities for growth that are essential for a thriving marriage.

ENJOYING MINISTRY TOGETHER

Marriage itself is a ministry. Couples are called to serve God not only within their home but also in their community and church. Finding a joint ministry allows couples to combine their talents and passions in service to God. This shared mission can bring immense fulfillment and joy, as they witness the impact of their united efforts.

Serving together in ministry also helps couples understand and appreciate each other's spiritual gifts. It fosters a sense of unity and collaboration, deepening their relationship and enhancing their ability to work as a team.

BATTLING THE ENEMY'S ATTACKS

The enemy does not want marriages to express God's glory on earth. Therefore, he targets the covenant vows made by couples. By fostering a strong prayer life and actively participating in church, couples can fortify their marriage against these attacks. They must remain vigilant and committed to their vows, understanding that their union is a testament to God's love and purpose.

In conclusion, viewing marriage as God's product and a ministry transforms how couples approach their union. By actively involving God in their marriage, serving together in ministry, and staying connected to their church, couples can build a strong, resilient marriage that fulfills God's purpose and withstands the enemy's attacks.

Serving in the Church and Community
THE CALL TO SERVE

Serving in the church and community is a fundamental aspect of living out one's faith. For married couples, serving together not only strengthens their bond but also allows them to fulfill their God-given purpose. The Bible emphasizes the importance of service and highlights that believers are called to be the hands and feet of Christ in the world. **1 Peter 4:10 states, "As each has received a gift, use it to serve one another, as good stewards of God's varied grace."** This scripture underlines the principle that each person has unique gifts and talents, and they should use these gifts to serve others. For couples, this means finding ways to use their combined talents to benefit their church and community.

- **Understanding the Call:** The call to serve is a fundamental aspect of the Christian faith. Service is not merely an optional activity but a core expression of living out one's faith and embodying the teachings of Jesus Christ. For married couples, the call to serve is an invitation to work together in fulfilling God's purposes on earth. This call is rooted in the understanding that each believer has been gifted by God with unique talents and abilities that are meant to be used for the benefit of others and the glory of God. **Ephesians 2:10** says, **"For we are his workmanship, created in Christ Jesus for good works, which God prepared beforehand, that we should walk in them."** This verse highlights that believers are created for good works and that these works are part of God's plan for their lives. For couples, this means recognizing that their marriage is not just for their own enjoyment but also for serving God and others.

- **Serving Together as a Couple:** Serving together as a couple can have a profound impact on both the marriage and the community. It allows couples to combine their strengths, support each other in their weaknesses, and grow together in their faith. Joint service can also help couples develop a deeper understanding of each other's gifts and how they complement each other. **Ecclesiastes 4:9-10** states, **"Two are better than one, because they have a good reward for their labor. For if they fall, one will lift up his companion. But woe to him who is alone when he falls, for he has no one to help him up."** This passage underscores the importance of partnership and mutual support, which are essential in both marriage and service.

- **Reflecting Christ's Love:** When couples serve together, they reflect Christ's love to those they serve and to the wider community. Their joint efforts can serve as a powerful witness to the transformative power of the Gospel and the beauty of a Christ-centered marriage. By serving others, couples can demonstrate the selflessness, compassion, and love that are hallmarks of the Christian faith. **Matthew 5:16** encourages believers to, **"Let your light shine before others, that they may see your good deeds and glorify your Father in heaven."** Through their service, couples can shine the light of Christ and bring glory to God.

- **Discovering Joint Ministry:** Every couple has a unique joint ministry, a specific way in which God has called them to serve together. Discovering this joint ministry involves prayer, reflection, and a willingness to step out in faith. Couples should seek God's guidance to understand how they can best use their combined gifts and talents to serve Him and others in their local church community. **Romans 12:4-5** explains, **"For just as each of us has one body with many members, and these members do not all have the same function, so in Christ we, though many, form one body, and each member belongs to all the others."** This passage highlights the diversity of gifts within the body of Christ and the importance of each member's contribution. For couples, finding their joint ministry means identifying how their unique gifts complement each other and how they can best serve the body of Christ together.

- **Building a Legacy of Service:** By serving together, couples can build a legacy of service that will inspire future generations. Their commitment to service can influence their children, family members, and others in their community. This legacy of service can have a lasting impact, encouraging others to live out their faith through acts of love and service. **Proverbs 22:6** advises, **"Train up a child in the way he should go, and when he is old he will not depart from it."** When children see their parents serving together, they learn the value of service and are more likely to adopt this mindset in their own lives.

- **The Joy of Serving:** Serving together can bring immense joy and fulfillment. It allows couples to experience the joy of making a difference in the lives of others and seeing the impact of their efforts. This joy can deepen their bond and create lasting memories that strengthen their relationship. **Acts 20:35 reminds us, "In everything I did, I showed you that by this kind of hard work we must help the weak, remembering the words the Lord Jesus himself said: 'It is more blessed to give than to receive"** The act of giving and serving brings a unique blessing and joy that enriches both the giver and the recipient.

The call to serve is a vital aspect of the Christian life and marriage. By serving together, couples can strengthen their bond, reflect Christ's love, discover their joint ministry, build a legacy of service, overcome challenges, and experience the joy of making a difference. Embracing the call to serve allows couples to live out their faith in a meaningful way and fulfill God's purposes for their marriage.

STRENGTHENING MARITAL BONDS

Serving together provides couples with opportunities to work as a team, fostering cooperation, communication, and mutual support. When couples engage in service, they learn to rely on each other's strengths, address each other's weaknesses, and grow together in their faith. This collaborative effort can enhance their relationship and create a deeper sense of unity. **Ecclesiastes 4:9-10** highlights the power of partnership: **"Two are better than one, because they have a good return for their labor: If either of them falls down, one can help the other up. But pity anyone who falls and has no one to help them up."** Serving together embodies this principle, as couples support and uplift each other through their joint efforts.

REFLECTING CHRIST'S LOVE

By serving in the church and community, couples can reflect Christ's love and compassion to those around them. Their service acts as a living testimony of their faith and commitment to God's work. Whether it's through volunteering at a local food bank, mentoring young couples, or participating in church outreach programs, their actions can inspire others and bring glory to God.

Matthew 5:16 encourages believers to, **"Let your light shine before others, that they may see your good deeds and glorify your Father in heaven."** When couples serve together, they become a beacon of Christ's love, demonstrating the transformative power of a life devoted to service.

OVERCOMING CHALLENGES

Serving together can present challenges, such as differing opinions on where and how to serve, balancing service with other commitments, and managing the emotional and physical demands of service. However, overcoming these challenges can strengthen a marriage and deepen the couple's faith.

Open communication and mutual respect are crucial in navigating these challenges. Couples should regularly discuss their service commitments, share their feelings and concerns, and seek to understand each other's perspectives. Prayer and reliance on God's guidance can also help couples stay aligned and focused on their joint ministry.

Philippians 2:3-4 advises. **"Do nothing out of selfish ambition or vain conceit. Rather, in humility value others above yourselves, not looking to your own interests but each of you to the interests of the others."** This mindset is essential for couples to serve effectively together, as it encourages selflessness and prioritizing the needs of others.

IMPACTING THE COMMUNITY

When couples serve together, their impact on the community can be significant. Their combined efforts can bring about positive change, provide much-needed support to those in need, and foster a sense of community and belonging. Their service can also serve as a powerful witness to the transformative power of Christ's love and the strength of a united marriage. **Galatians 6:9-10** encourages perseverance in doing good: **"Let us not become weary in doing good, for at the proper time we will reap a harvest if we do not give up. Therefore, as we have opportunity, let us do good to all people, especially to those who belong to the family of believers."** This exhortation reminds couples of the lasting impact of their service and the importance of persisting in their efforts.

Serving in the church and community is a vital aspect of a Christ-centered marriage. It strengthens marital bonds, reflects Christ's love, helps couples discover their joint ministry, and positively impacts the community. By overcoming challenges together and committing to a life of service, couples can grow in their faith, support each other, and fulfill their God-given purpose.

Renewing Your Vows and Commitment
THE IMPORTANCE OF RENEWAL

Renewing your vows and commitment is a powerful way to reaffirm the promises made on your wedding day. It serves as a reminder of the love and dedication shared between partners and strengthens the bond of marriage. Over time, the challenges and demands of life can cause couples to drift apart or lose sight of the initial commitment. A vow renewal ceremony provides an opportunity to refocus on each other and the marriage.

Revelation 2:4-5 says. **"Yet I hold this against you: You have forsaken the love you had at first. Consider how far you have fallen! Repent and do the things you did at first."** This verse encourages believers to remember and rekindle their first love, a principle that can be applied to marriage as well.

WHEN TO RENEW VOWS

There is no set time for renewing vows; it can be done at any point in a marriage. Some couples choose to renew their vows on significant anniversaries, such as the 10th, 25th, or 50th, while others may do so after overcoming a challenging period or simply when they feel the need to reaffirm their commitment.

The decision to renew vows should be mutual and heartfelt. It is an opportunity for both partners to express their continued love and dedication in a meaningful and sincere manner.

PLANNING A VOW RENEWAL CEREMONY

Planning a vow renewal ceremony can be as simple or elaborate as the couple desires. It can be a private, intimate affair or a larger celebration with family and friends. The focus should be on the couple and their commitment to each other.

- **Choosing a Location**: The location can be a meaningful place for the couple, such as the church where they were married, a favorite vacation spot, or their home. The setting should reflect the couple's personality and the significance of the occasion.

- **Writing Vows**: Couples can write new vows or revisit and revise their original ones. The vows should reflect their journey together, the growth in their relationship, and their hopes for the future. Writing personalized vows allows each partner to express their love and commitment in their own words.

- **Involving Loved Ones**: Involving children, family members, and close friends can make the ceremony more special. They can participate by reading scripture, sharing memories, or offering blessings and prayers for the couple.

- **Symbolic Gestures**: Including symbolic gestures, such as lighting a unity candle, pouring of unity sand, exchanging new rings, or planting a tree, can add depth and meaning to the ceremony. These acts symbolize the ongoing growth and unity of the marriage.

REAFFIRMING COMMITMENT

Renewing vows is not just about repeating words; it is about reaffirming the commitment to love, honor, and cherish each other. It is a time to reflect on the journey so far, acknowledge the challenges overcome, and look forward to the future together.

1 Corinthians 13:4-7 provides a timeless description of love: **"Love is patient, love is kind. It does not envy, it does not boast, it is not proud. It does not dishonor others, it is not self-seeking, it is not easily angered, it keeps no record of wrongs. Love does not delight in evil but rejoices with the truth. It always protects, always trusts, always hopes, always perseveres."** These verses can serve as a guide for the renewed commitment.

RENEWING SPIRITUAL COMMITMENT

A vow renewal ceremony is also an opportunity to renew spiritual commitment. Couples can reaffirm their dedication to growing in their faith together, supporting each other in their spiritual journeys, and keeping God at the center of their marriage. **Joshua 24:15 states, "But as for me and my household, we will serve the Lord."** This declaration can serve as an inspiration for couples to renew their commitment to serving God as a family.

Celebrating Milestones

Celebrating milestones in a marriage, such as a vow renewal, can provide a sense of achievement and gratitude. It allows couples to acknowledge and celebrate the strength and resilience of their relationship. Reflecting on the journey and the milestones achieved can bring a renewed sense of purpose and joy.

MOVING FORWARD

After renewing their vows, couples should continue to nurture their relationship. Regularly expressing love and appreciation, maintaining open communication, and spending quality time together are essential for a healthy and thriving marriage. The renewal ceremony is a reminder to keep the commitment alive in everyday actions and decisions. **Philippians 3:13-14** encourages believers to press on: **"Forgetting what is behind and straining toward what is ahead, I press on toward the goal to win the prize for which God has called me heavenward in Christ Jesus."** This mindset can be applied to marriage, encouraging couples to look forward with hope and determination.

Renewing your vows and commitment is a significant and meaningful act that can strengthen the bond between spouses. It is an opportunity to reflect on the journey, celebrate the growth, and look forward to the future together. By reaffirming their love and dedication, couples can deepen their connection and ensure their marriage continues to thrive with God's guidance and blessings.

CONCLUSION

EMBRACING THE JOURNEY

Conclusion
Embracing the Journey

Marriage is not just a destination but a continuous journey of learning, growth, adaptation, and deepening connection. From the moment you say "I do," you embark on an adventure that encompasses both joyous highs and challenging lows, each shaping and strengthening your bond.

Philippians 1:6 reassures us. **"Being confident of this, that he who began a good work in you will carry it on to completion until the day of Christ Jesus."** Embrace the journey with confidence, knowing that every experience, whether blissful or difficult, is part of God's plan for your union.

EACH SEASON OF MARRIAGE BRINGS UNIQUE OPPORTUNITIES FOR GROWTH

- **Spring (New Beginnings)**: Establish strong communication habits and set a shared vision for your future.

    Job 8:7 (KJV) And though your start was small, your end will be very great.

- **Summer (Growth and Abundance)**: Deepen your emotional and spiritual connection, and celebrate milestones together.

    Joel 2:21 (KJV) Fear not, O land; be glad and rejoice: for the Lord will do great things.

- **Autumn (Change and Transition)**: Navigate life's transitions together, finding new ways to connect.

    2Cor 4:16 (BBE) For which because we do not give way to weariness; but though our outer man is getting feebler, our inner man is made new day by day.

- **Winter (Reflection and Renewal)**: Reflect on your journey and renew your commitment to each other.

Deut 31:6 Be strong and of good courage, fear not, nor be afraid of them: for the Lord thy God, he [it is] that doth go with thee; he will not fail thee, nor forsake thee.

Challenges are inevitable, but they are opportunities for growth and deeper understanding. **James 1:2-4 advises, "Consider it pure joy, my brothers and sisters, whenever you face trials of many kinds, because you know that the testing of your faith produces perseverance."** Face challenges together, knowing they build resilience and maturity in your relationship.

Celebrate your milestones and achievements, and recognize the importance of building a lasting legacy. **Psalm 127:1** highlights the importance of relying on God to build and sustain your marriage: **"Unless the Lord builds the house, the builders labor in vain."** Your relationship serves as a model for future generations, demonstrating love, respect, and commitment.

CONTINUAL DEPENDENCE ON GOD

A fulfilling marriage requires continual dependence on God, who is the source of love, strength, wisdom, and guidance. Keep God at the center of your relationship to ensure a solid foundation. Regular prayer, scripture reading, and church attendance are essential practices that help maintain this dependence.

Proverbs 3:5-6 advises, **"Trust in the Lord with all your heart and lean not on your own understanding; in all your ways submit to him, and he will make your paths straight."** This underscores the importance of relying on God's wisdom and guidance in all aspects of your marriage.

Encourage each other's spiritual growth by making time for joint worship and prayer. These spiritual disciplines not only draw you closer to God but also strengthen your bond with each other. When challenges arise, turn to God for strength and direction, allowing His peace to guard your hearts.

ENCOURAGEMENT FOR THE ROAD AHEAD

The journey of marriage is filled with both ups and downs, but with God's grace, each moment can be used for growth and deeper connection. As you look to the future, take heart in knowing that you are not alone. God is with you every step of the way, providing support and encouragement.

Mt 19:6 Wherefore they are no more twain, but one flesh. What therefore God hath joined together, let not man put asunder.

Mt 19:7 They say unto him, why did Moses then command to give a writing of divorcement, and to put her away?

Mt 19:8 He saith unto them, Moses because of the hardness of your hearts suffered you to put away your wives: but from the beginning it was not so.

- **Cherish the Moments**: Make a habit of appreciating the small, everyday moments that build your relationship. Express gratitude for your partner and be intentional about creating memories.

- **Stay Committed**: Commitment is the bedrock of a strong marriage. Dedicate yourselves to each other and to the vows you made, allowing this steadfastness to see you through difficult times and enhance your joy during good times.

- **Communicate Openly**: Maintain open and honest communication. Share your thoughts, feelings, and concerns with empathy and understanding. Healthy communication is essential for resolving conflicts and building trust.

- **Support Each Other's Dreams**: Encourage each other to pursue personal and shared dreams. Be each other's biggest cheerleader and source of support. When both partners feel valued and supported, the marriage thrives.

- **Seek Continuous Improvement**: Never stop learning and growing together. Attend marriage seminars, read books on relationships, and seek counsel from mentors who can provide wisdom and guidance. Embrace opportunities for personal and relational development.

In conclusion, embracing the journey of marriage means committing to a lifelong process of growth, love, and partnership. By depending on God, cherishing each moment, and supporting each other, you can build a strong, enduring marriage that reflects God's love and grace in, and for your generation.

Pss 52:9 I will praise thee forever, because thou hast done [it]: and I will wait on thy name; for [it is] good before thy saints.

Scriptural Prayers for Couples to Pray Together

Colossians   3:14
And above all these things put on charity, which is the bond of perfectness.

Prayer:
Holy Spirit, may the love of God overtake every part of our being, binding us together in perfect unity.

Colossians   3:9
Lie not one to another, seeing that ye have put off the old man with his deeds.

Prayer:
Lord Jesus, we bind every lie that has crept into our marriage and ask for Your truth to reign.

Colossians   3:8
But now ye also put off all these; anger, wrath, malice, blasphemy, filthy communication out of your mouth.

Prayer:
Lord Jesus, by the power of Your Holy Spirit, we cast out every trace of anger, malice, and bitterness that seeks to divide us.

Job   34:32
That which I see not teach thou me: if I have done iniquity, I will do no more.

Prayer:
Holy Spirit, reveal to me the areas where I fall short in our marriage, so I may begin to grow in those areas.

James   1:4
But let patience have her perfect work, that ye may be perfect and entire, wanting nothing.

Prayer:
Father God, grant me patience in our marriage, especially as I wait for my spouse to grow in the areas where they need it.

James 2:26

For as the body without the spirit is dead, so faith without works is dead also.

Prayer:

Holy Spirit, inspire us to actively apply practical changes that will strengthen our marriage.

---

1 Corinthians 1:10

Now I beseech you, brethren, by the name of our Lord Jesus Christ, that ye all speak the same thing, and that there be no divisions among you; but that ye be perfectly joined together in the same mind and in the same judgment.

Prayer:

Holy Spirit, we bind the spirit of division in our marriage. Help us to be unified in spirit, body, and soul in all things.

Ephesians 5:21

Submitting yourselves one to another in the fear of God.

Prayer:

Lord Jesus, may You alone be our motivation as we submit to one another in love and reverence.

Ephesians 5:29

For no man ever yet hated his own flesh; but nourisheth and cherisheth it, even as the Lord the church:

Prayer:

Lord Jesus, give me the courage and heart to invest time, knowledge, and selfless care into my spouse.

Colossians 3:18

Wives, submit yourselves unto your own husbands, as it is fit in the Lord.

Prayer:

Holy Spirit, help me to respect and honor my spouse, not because they are perfect, but because it pleases You, Lord.

Colossians 3:21
Fathers, provoke not your children to anger, lest they be discouraged.

Prayer:
Holy Spirit, convict us as parents when we provoke or discourage our children, and guide us to lead with love.

Psalm 25:4
Make your steps clear to me, O Lord; give me knowledge of your ways.

Prayer:
Father God, show us Your ways and reveal Your wisdom to us concerning our marriage so we may reflect Your glory.

Matthew 18:19
Again I say unto you, That if two of you shall agree on earth as touching anything that they shall ask, it shall be done for them of my Father which is in heaven.

Prayer:
Holy Spirit, empower us to stand together in prayer, especially in times of trouble.

Proverbs 31:26
She openeth her mouth with wisdom; and in her tongue is the law of kindness.

Prayer:
Holy Spirit, help me to speak words of wisdom and kindness in our marriage, towards my spouse and children.

Proverbs 1:5
A wise man will hear, and will increase learning; and a man of understanding shall attain unto wise counsels.

Prayer:
Lord Jesus, help me to walk in wisdom by listening and applying the godly counsel given by my spouse.

---

1 **Peter** 5:10
But the God of all grace, who hath called us unto his eternal glory by Christ Jesus, after that ye have suffered a while, make you perfect, stablish, strengthen, settle you.

Prayer:
Father God, though our marriage has faced challenges, we thank You for perfecting, establishing, strengthening, and settling us in Your glory.

---

1 Corinthians   **11:3**
But I would have you know, that the head of every man is Christ; and the head of the woman is the man; and the head of Christ is God.

Prayer:
Holy Spirit, help us to always follow the divine order in our marriage.

Isaiah   **54:17**
No weapon that is formed against thee shall prosper; and every tongue that shall rise against thee in judgment thou shalt condemn. This is the heritage of the servants of the Lord, and their righteousness is of me, saith the Lord.

Prayer:
Lord Jesus, we decree that no weapon formed against our marriage shall prosper—no division, no sickness, no threats of divorce, no spiritual attacks.

Ephesians   **4:27**
Neither give place to the devil.

Prayer:
Lord, we stand together in the mighty name of Jesus to close every door where we've allowed the enemy to enter our marriage.

Proverbs   **18:21**
Death and life are in the power of the tongue: and they that love it shall eat the fruit thereof.

Prayer:
Lord Jesus, we speak life over our marriage—peace, joy, love, financial wisdom, healing, faithfulness, and generational blessings.

Numbers   **14:21**
But as truly as I live, all the earth shall be filled with the glory of the Lord.

Prayer:
Holy Spirit, may our marriage reflect the character, nature, and integrity of our Heavenly Father.

Ephesians 5:31-32
For this cause shall a man leave his father and mother, and shall be joined unto his wife, and they two shall be one flesh. This is a great mystery: but I speak concerning Christ and the church.

Prayer:
Lord Jesus, may our marriage be the greatest sermon ever preached, leaving a legacy of love and faith for generations to come.

Hosea 4:6
My people are destroyed for lack of knowledge: because thou hast rejected knowledge, I will also reject thee.

Prayer:
Holy Spirit, give us the strength and desire to seek Your knowledge, that our marriage may thrive in the areas where we struggle.

---

1 **Corinthians** **7:5**
"Defraud ye not one the other, except it be with consent for a time, that ye may give yourselves to fasting and prayer; and come together again, that Satan tempts you not for your incontinence."

Prayer **Point:**
Lord Jesus, help us to not defraud one another selfishly and ignorantly in our marriage. Lord, forgive us for allowing Satan to tempt our spouse due to our inconsistency.

THE KINGDOM MANUAL FOR A VICTORIOUS LIVING

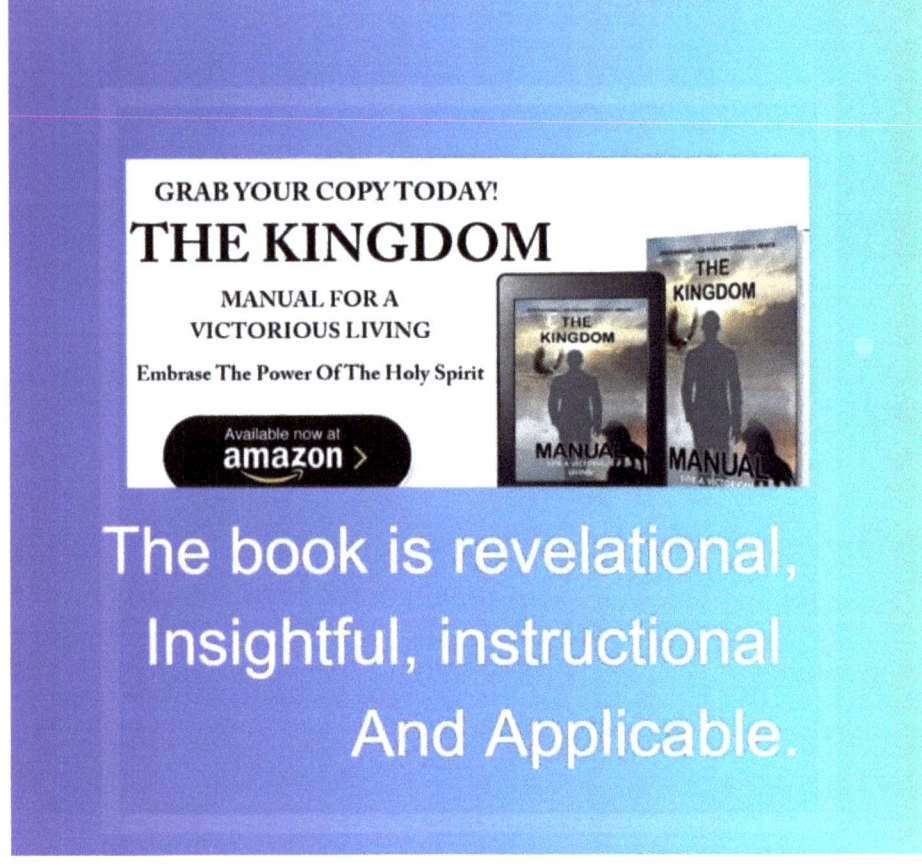

The Victorious Kingdom Manual" is a sacred journey penned with divine inspiration and sincerity, a testament to timeless truths that resonate across generations. Crafted by Prophetess and her co-author with singular and fervent prayers, this manual unfolds as a transformative experience, ignited by the Spirit of the Living God.

Kindly get your copy on Amazon today; https://shorturl.at/Z2bhm

www.ingramcontent.com/pod-product-compliance
Lightning Source LLC
LaVergne TN
LVHW050131080526
838202LV00061B/6465